COUNTRY COUS

CONTENTS

INTRODUCTION

Following the inception of the London Passenger Transport Board in 1933, not only were bus, tram and trolleybus services within Greater London taken over by the new authority, but so were those within approximately a forty-mile radius of Charing Cross in the counties of Middlesex, Hertfordshire, Essex, Kent, Surrey, Sussex, Berkshire, Buckinghamshire and Bedfordshire.

These areas became the Board's Country Area, and the buses operated therein adopted a livery of Lincoln Green and cream in distinct contrast to the red and cream of their counterparts in Greater London, whose operating area became the Central Area. With the Country Area bus services also went the Green Line coach network, which operated many cross-London services, for example from Tunbridge Wells to Windsor, and from Hertford to Guildford. At the time of the LPTB takeover, Country and Green Line services already had much in common with their Central Area counterparts - most of the latter were taken over from the London General Omnibus Company, which had a 'Country Area' subsidiary London General Country Services and had also initiated the Green Line coach network a few years previously.

The LPTB quickly established a corporate image, adopting the name 'London Transport' and the 'bullseye' symbol which had already been used by the LGOC and much of the Underground railway system since before the First World War. Standard LT bus stop flags would soon be seen everywhere from Hitchin to Crawley and from Windsor to Tilbury, and it was the same with the buses themselves. Wherever possible, standardised bus and coach types were introduced, particularly in the Country Area which inherited a very motley fleet of vehicles. Sadly interrupted by World War Two, this process reached a peak of standardisation in the mid-1950s, by which time more than 7,000 RT-type double-deckers and 700 RF single-deckers had become THE motor buses for the whole of the London Transport system - red for the Central Area and green for the Country Area: the latter were indeed the 'Country Cousins' of the more numerous red London buses!

By the time the first of my photographs in this new volume were taken, the London Transport Country Area had existed for almost thirty years. Unfortunately, due to the policies of Harold Wilson's Labour government, the Country buses and Green Line coaches were split off from London Transport (control of which passed to the Greater London Council) on 1st January 1970. They were formed into London Country Bus Services Ltd, a subsidiary of the National Bus Company which itself had absorbed many traditional bus companies throughout England and Wales a couple of years beforehand. However, for several years, the new London Country fleet was still largely made up of former London Transport types, and indeed it was not until a full decade later that their last ex-LT buses were withdrawn. The LT legacy lasted longer than that, in that many of the traditional bus routes and the garages that operated them survived until even after London Country was first split up into four geographical segments, and then privatised by the Thatcher regime in the 1980s. Even today some of the old routes survive, along with a handful of their operating garages.

In this volume I have selected a number of my photographs of London Transport Country Area and London Country buses and Green Line coaches taken during the last decade of LT operation, and until the final split-up into the four London Country successor operators in 1986. They cover a time period of almost twenty-five years and illustrate not only the familiar standard London Transport vehicles of the RT, RF and RM families, but also the minority GS and RLH classes of the LT years, the new one-man-operated vehicles of the final LT era and the host of different classes introduced under London Country auspices. The photographs are presented in chronological order. This is by no means intended to be a full historical record of the Country and Green Line routes: that would require a much bigger volume than this and, besides, has been adequately done before!

All of the photographs are my own, and many have not been published before. My thanks go to the PSV Circle and London Omnibus Traction Society on whose records some of the historical details are based, also to Colin Clarke who painstakingly scanned all of my original negatives over some six years or so and to publisher Ken Carr for making this volume possible!

Jim Blake
Palmers Green
1st September 2017

This book is dedicated to all the friends I travelled around with in the years the photo's herein were taken, in particular George Ledger, Jeremy Buck, Jim Owen, Pete Horner and Tony Wolton. They often drove me around pursuing them, enabling me to photograph much more than if I had travelled on the buses themselves!

Front Cover Photo: In the final stages of crew operation for London Country, RCL2242 (CM) stands outside its home garage, Chelsham on 23rd August 1978. Interestingly, it has an upper-case number and via blind produced specially for the RCLs here at this late stage, but it is unfortunately torn! Two years later, this RCL would be one of the first to work as a red bus following its return to London Transport.

Rear Cover Photo: Exemplifying the very shoddy state London Country's Routemasters were in in their final years, RML2336 (NF) loads up at Horns Cross on route 480 in the evening rush hour of 22nd September 1978.

Many Country Area bus routes served New Towns in the Home Counties which were established in the early postwar years to resettle people who had been bombed out in London during the war. A typical example was Stevenage, in whose New Town centre bus station RT1026 (SV) is working Town Service 392 on Thursday, 9th August 1962. Such services were later numbered in the 800 series, and RTs would survive on them here for another ten years. I often visited this town, having had relatives resettled there from Highbury in 1956.

Stevenage New Town is situated directly south of the Old Town on the Great North Road. On the same day as the previous picture, RF173 (SV) calls at the bus station on the long Green Line coach route 716, running all the way from Hitchin to Chertsey. This coach was ten years old at the time, and would be modernised five years later ensuring its survival well into the 1970s. However, RFs were replaced by new RMC coaches on the 716 and 716A in the winter of 1962/63.

Brand new Routemaster Green Line coach RMC1463 (GF) approaches Manor House Station on route 715, on Wednesday, 29th August 1962 the first day of service for this class. The RMC makes an interesting contrast with the standard red RM following on route 269, whilst a British Railways van completes the picture. However, all 68 of the RMC coaches, along with the prototype RMC4, had been demoted to Country bus operation by the spring of 1972. From the end of 1977, most were repurchased by London Transport and used as a driver trainers, though a few were returned to service in 1989 in red livery, lasting until 2003.

Left: In complete contrast to the RTs, RFs and Routemasters which comprised most of the Country Area fleet in the 1960s was the GS class. These were 26-seat Guy Specials with E.C.W. bodywork, intended for use on lightly-used routes, or routes with restrictive clearances that could not accommodate larger buses. 84 of them were built in 1953/54 to replace the similar-sized pre-war C and CR classes of Leyland Cubs. However, even by 7th April 1964 when GS39 (DS) is operating route 433 in Dorking Bus Station, withdrawals of this non-standard class had already begun, due either to service cuts or their replacement by RFs.

Below: Whereas from 1952 until 1965, the majority of Green Line coach routes were operated by RFs, a number of busy Green Line routes which ran from Aldgate to South West Essex were operated by RTs. These were the 721 and 722 based at Romford, London Road Garage and the 723, 723A and 723B at Grays. On 11th May 1965, RT3254 (RE) stands at Aldgate, Minories Bus Station on route 722. During the next couple of months, all of these RTs, which apart from being adorned in the standard Green Line livery of Lincoln green with a light green waistband and raised 'Green Line' bullseyes between decks were no different from ordinary Country RTs, were replaced by new RCL class long Routemaster coaches. Use of the latter on the 722 was short-lived, however, since RTs returned to it in 1966 and the route was discontinued the following year. Meanwhile, the RTs on these routes were all demoted to bus status. This particular one was one of two repurchased by London Transport in 1972; which lasted until the end in 1979 and both are preserved today, this one in Green Line livery.

Above: Standard Country Area RTs often worked as Green Line reliefs when the need arose. On 6th June 1965, RT626 (SV) lays over at Stevenage Garage, which was just across the road from the bus station seen earlier, between turns on route 716.

Right: When the first Dartford Tunnel opened in the autumn of 1963, new Country bus route 300 was introduced running through it using RTs, and Green Line route 722 was extended from Corbets Tey to Dartford as well, also with them. However, both were little used, and by 27th June 1965 when GS28 (GY) was standing at Grays War Memorial terminus, these little 26-seaters on new limited stop route 399 to Dartford were deemed adequate for the few passengers who travelled by bus through the tunnel. And even this route did not last long!

Three days after entering experimental service, brand new XF8 (EG) picks up passengers in Bell Street, Reigate on 21st September 1965. There were eight of these Park Royal-bodied Daimler Fleetlines, which had virtually identical bodies to fifty Leyland Atlanteans being tried out in the Central Area. Between 1966 and 1969, they were actually exchanged with eight of these on routes 271 and 67 for comparative trials. A novel feature of these XFs was that their upper decks could be sealed off at quiet times to enable them to be one-man-operated as 'single-deckers'; OMO working of double-deckers not then being permitted. A handful of XFs remained on route 424 into the early 1980s, being some of the last ex-London Transport buses operated by London Country.

Saturday, 5th March 1966 is market day in St. Albans, where RF587 (SA) has just loaded up in busy St. Peters Street on route 355. The entire batch of Country bus RFs originally built as such in 1953, RF539-700, along with all those that were converted from Green Line coaches in the mid-1960s, survived to be taken over by London Country, and many lasted well into the 1970s. A tribute to their sound and sturdy design!

On the evening of the same day, RT2700 (GR) has run into Garston Garage after working route 347. This RT is one of many overhauled green ex-red in the winter of 1963/64 with early RT3/1 bodies to replace the last roofbox RTs in the Country Area. Soon after this picture was taken, RTs on route 347, and route 311 on which the RT behind has been working, will be replaced by new RMLs. Paradoxically, many of the RTs thus displaced were overhauled red ex-green to replace RTLs and RTWs in the Central Area!

In the summer of 1966, after much delay, a new northern orbital Green Line Express route 724 was introduced, linking Romford and High Wycombe via such places as Harlow, Hertford, St. Albans and Watford. On 10th September 1966, RF138 (RE) collects passengers in the bus station at Harlow, another of the post-war New Towns. An RT on Town Service 804 stands behind it.

Also at Harlow Bus Station that day is RML2458 (HA), one of the second batch of fifty RMLs delivered to replace RTs on busy Country Area routes during the winter of 1965/66. Curiously, RMLs and RTs worked Harlow Town Services together for some time after this. Some of the Country RTs displaced by these new RMLs were also overhauled in red to replace RTLs and RTWs in the Central Area, effectively finishing the latter off. Sadly, this RML was one of seventeen that were cannibalised as a result of the mid-1970s vehicle spares shortage, and scrapped in 1978. All but two other Country RMLs were repurchased by London Transport and lasted at London's service until 2003-2005.

By the autumn of 1966, most of the low-height RLHs remaining in the Country area were based at Addlestone and Guildford Garages, needed for busy routes that passed beneath the many low railway bridges in the area. On 30th October 1966, RLH24 (GF) stands at the entrance of Guildford Garage, ready to run out on route 436. This was one of the second batch of these Weymann-bodied A.E.C. Regent IIIs, new in 1952.

Route 471 was one of a couple of cases on which GSs could be seen on the 'borderlands' between the Central and Country Areas. On a drizzly 19th November 1966, GS56 (DS) stands at Orpington Station on the circular route 471, which served the quaintly-named village of Pratts Bottom. Of note is the knob protruding from the nearside wing of the GS - this is a 'kerb-guide' aimed at helping the driver to avoid scuffing its tyres on kerbs of narrow roads. The RT in the background is a red one terminating on route 229. GSs were not really needed on the 471; RFs subsequently replaced them.

Later on the same day, RT1616 (DG) stands in a soggy Sevenoaks Bus Station en route to Tonbridge on route 454. This was the extremity of Country Area bus operation in that area, though Green Line coaches continued further (on route 704) to Tunbridge Wells, where they also had a small garage.

On a very wet Whit Saturday, 27th May 1967, RLH14 passes through Woking bound for Guildford on route 463. By now, this was one of the only two remaining RLH's of the first batch of twenty. These were delivered in 1950 and were a diverted order from Midland General. RLHs had Weymann bodywork, built in Addlestone very close to the Country Area Garage in that town where many were actually based.

On 3rd June 1967, RLH45 (WY) passes Woking Station on route 436A bound for Ripley. Many of the low bridges in this area which enforced RLH operation were on the London & South Western main line, on which this station was situated. At the time this picture was taken, I was in the area filming the last steam engines on the Southern Region, which were withdrawn just five weeks later. This RLH is one of the second batch of 56, built in 1952.

On Derby Day, 7th June 1967, RT4113 (GD) is on loan to Godstone Garage working special route 406F, and disgorges racegoers at Epsom Downs. Of note is the advertisement between decks on the offside, promoting the newly-introduced Green Line Airport Express route 727, which linked Luton, Heathrow and Gatwick Airports. This RT was another of the 34 bought back by London Transport in September 1972.

Country Area and Green Line vehicles worked excursions to Epsom Downs for The Derby. RT3081 accompanies RF139, both from Luton Garage. The RT carries an odd livery with a green waistband and a white fleetname, but contrary to what many people thought at the time was not a former Green Line RT - it had in fact originally been red. The RF is one of the recently modernised Green Line examples.

In 1960, several Country RTs were painted in Green Line livery to act as reliefs during rush hours or bank holidays. One was RT613 (HG) which passes Marble Arch in the evening of 11th July 1967, long after the 715 had received RMCs. The fact that it has an RM side-blind in the front, rather than a 'Green Line Relief' display suggests that it might be covering for RMCs which were having their first Aldenham overhauls. These 'new' Green Line RTs could be distinguished from the original ones at Grays and Romford by having only a painted 'Green Line' bullseye between decks, rather than a raised one. This may be discerned here.

At a very wet Watford Junction Station on 21st October 1967, recently modernised RF66 (SA) has just called on the new 727 Green Line Express. It is revealing that fifteen or sixteen-year-old RFs were used on this, rather than newer vehicles. However, their modernisation, which involved new twin-headlamps, a deep, light-green waistband, fluorescent lighting and seat moquette and interior trim in the same style as the recently-built Routemaster coaches, was so convincing that many people thought they were new! Needless to say, it was carried out in-house at Aldenham Works. In common with the others used initially on the 727, this RF seated only 35 passengers as its rear four seats were removed to make way for extra luggage racks.

An oddity on the stand at Watford Junction on the same occasion is RF553 (MA), about to depart for Chesham on route 336. As the brackets above its side windows show, this Country Bus RF carries a body originally on a Green Line RF. A handful of such combinations arose in the mid-1960s when a batch of Green Line RFs were demoted to bus status, and went through Aldenham overhaul at the same time that the overhaul cycle for RFs which had always been Country buses began, and bodies became intermixed.

In common with most London Transport buses in the 1960s, overhauls of Country Area buses and Green Line coaches were carried out at LT's huge Aldenham Works. On 9th November 1967, the body of what will emerge a few days later as Country RT3867 has just been mounted onto its chassis during overhaul there. Of note is the new one-piece curved panel beneath its windscreen, a part of these buses that was for some reason particularly prone to knocks and bumps. Spare panels such as these were kept at Aldenham, both for use during overhaul and for accident damage repairs. On the left, a Green Line RMC coach is undergoing its first overhaul.

Sporting the revised Green Line livery that omitted the light green beading around the windows, RMC1514 has just had its first overhaul and awaits being taken into Aldenham's famous 'oven', where the new paintwork was varnished to keep it good for the next three or four years. A standard red RM awaits the same treatment behind it.

In the autumn of 1965, a batch of fourteen Willowbrook-bodied A.E.C. Reliances, the RC class, was delivered to London Transport for evaluation as possible replacements for the RFs on Green Line coach services. They operated route 705 from Sevenoaks to Windsor, whose western section was limited stop via the M4 motorway. However, they were not a success. On their last day on this route, 29th November 1967, RC2 (DG) calls at Hyde Park Corner on its way west as daylight fades. As may be seen, the modernised RFs mimicked their appearance somewhat, though did not perpetuate their livery. The RCs in fact were repainted in the same two-tone Green Line livery as those RFs, seeing sporadic service, equally unsuccessfully, on routes 711, 725 and 727. In each case, they were replaced by RFs! They were finally demoted to Country bus work, and all withdrawn by 1978.

RCL class Routeamster coaches freed by reductions in their workload on the Aldgate routes replaced the RCs on route 705. Still in its original Green Line livery, RCL2242 (WR) races along the Bath Road, Harmondsworth on 10th March 1968.

Spring is near as RT4626 (LH) passes through Lower Kingswood on its way from Kingston to Redhill on the busy trunk route 406, the in-town section of which survives today. This RT is another formerly red RT with an RT3/1 body, due for withdrawal when this picture was taken on 16th March 1968.

Left: On the same day as the previous picture, red XA29 (EG) loads up in Bell Street, Reigate on route 424 whilst undergoing comparative trials with the eight green XFs at Stamford Hill already in exchange. At the time, I was annoyed at the Ford Anglia on the left obscuring part of the bus, but now, almost fifty years later, it adds to the 'period' atmopsher!

Below: Also on 16th March 1968, RT3900 (RG) has just changed crew outside Reigate Garage when working the long trunk route 414, which ran all the way from Horsham to West Croydon via Dorking. Note the splendid array of London Transport bus and Green Line coach timetables on the wall on the right! Reigate was the headquarters of London General Country Services Ltd before London Transport was set up, and played the same role for London Country Bus Services Ltd after the split with LT.

RF550 (HG) loads up in Hertford Bus Station on 30th March 1968 on route 350A, heading for Bishops Stortford, one of the furthest points from Central London that London Transport buses reached. A recently modernised Green Line RF on the northern peripheral route 724 is behind it.

Also at Hertford Bus Station that day, GS13 (HG) is working a very short journey back to Hertford Garage on route 308. This GS is one of many preserved today (who was it said that 97 out of the 84 GSs were preserved?!), which has appeared at 'running days' based on Hertford Bus Station in recent years. Unfortunately, today the bus station and surrounding buildings date only from the 1980s and 1990s, and are completely at odds with the 1940s, 1950s and 1960s buses at these events - this bus station shown in the pictures here is long gone!

On 30th March 1968, I travelled by RT on route 341 from Hertford to St. Albans, in whose St. Peter's Street, RT2999 (SA) collects shoppers from the nearby market on local route 325. The unusual 'lazy' via blind is of note, as is the rather crammed destination blind. This RT is another overhauled green ex-red with an early RT3/1 in 1963/64 to replace Country Area roofbox RTs. At this time, these were due for withdrawal, though in the event several of them survived well into the 1970s.

Two more of the ubiquitous RTs slosh through the rain in St. Peter's Street. RT3051 (LS) is in the lead, on the long trunk route 321 which ran all the way from Uxbridge to Luton, though usually in two overlapping sections. The second RT is on local route 361; a modernised Green Line RF completes the picture.

Left: The rain has got worse by the time I reach Hemel Hempstead on an RT on route 330. Unlike at Harlow and Stevenage, local Town Services for the New Town here were numbered in the normal northern Country Area series (300s) rather than in the 800s. RT2326 (HH), another ex-red RT3/1, is one of a handful of Country RTs that gained white fleetnames instead of gold ones upon overhaul or repaint in the summer of 1966, and passes the Market Square. The large LT 'bullseye' on the left points the way to Hemel Hempstead Bus Station.

Left: At the bus station itself, a very wet RF696 (HH) sets off for Berkhamsted on local route 317. For some reason, it is not showing its 'pay as you enter' slipboard below the front nearside window. This bus station also was the venue for vintage bus 'running days' in recent years, but unfortunately closed in 2016.

Below: Another RF in Hemel Hempstead that day is RF607 (HH), passing through the New Town centre on route 337 to Dunstable - another extremity of the northern Country Area of London Transport.

Above: From Hemel Hempstead, I travelled on an RML on route 347 to Garston Garage. This modern building, opened in 1952 to replace the older Watford High Street Garage, always had plenty of spare space which was used to store new or redundant vehicles. An oddity gathering dust there is RLH27, which some months earlier had been working from Reigate Garage. Some three months after this picture was taken, it was returned to service, still in green livery, on Central Area route 230 at Harrow Weald Garage, where it remained for almost a year. One of just three former LT Country Area garages still in use as this book is being compiled, Garston is sadly due to close in 2018.

Next day, 31st March 1968, I was back in the southern Country Area. Things are not as they seem with this RF on route 416 passing Leatherhead Station. Although those RFs built as Country Buses all originally had matching stock and registration numbers, owing to trials with one-man operation (to which eventually all were converted anyway) some were renumbered to keep the trial vehicles in a numerical block. Thus this RF is not RF698, as may be thought, but RF647 (LH)! Curiously, it is missing its 'pay as you enter' slipboard, too!

For some reason, a number of Country bus RFs did not receive an overhaul when due in 1968, having last been done in 1963. RF636 and RF638 (LH) were two of a few of them based at Leatherhead, where the garage is being rebuilt around them, also on 31st March 1968. Despite skipping an Aldenham overhaul, several of these RFs lasted well into the 1970s, in fact longer than some of those that were overhauled in 1968. By a remarkable coincidence, both RF636 and RT1700, on the extreme left of this picture, survive today in the heritage fleet of The London Bus Company Ltd!

On 6th April 1968, RT577 (HA) sets off from Harlow Bus Station on route 397 to Bishops Stortford. This RT, another one overhauled green ex-red with an early RT3/1 body to replace Country Area roofbox RTs in 1963/64, was the lowest-numbered postwar Country RT. The lowest-numbered newly-built as a Country Area green bus was RT597; roofbox RT593 preserved in green livery today was never green in service! Ironically, RT577 ended its days, still in green livery, as a staff bus at Putney Central Area Garage in 1970!

Left: In Harlow Bus Station itself, RML2453 (HA) accompanies one of its fellows working New Town Services for which they were sent there when new two years previously. Oddly enough, this RML also ended its days at Putney Garage, having operated as a red bus for some 25 years when finally withdrawn in July 2005!

Centre: My Green Rover on 6th April 1968 took me from Waltham Cross to Hertford, then to Harlow and Brentwood. From there, I had to take a Central Area (red) bus to Romford, where I resumed my trip by Country bus on a 370 to Tilbury. The British Railways ferry then took me across the river to Gravesend, where RT4193 (NF) works local route 498. Gravesend was a 'border town', where London Transport buses met those of Maidstone & District, one of whose Leyland Atlanteans passes the clocktower on the right. In the spring of 1969, this RT was replaced on local routes here by new MBSs. It was then overhauled in red to replace older roofbox RTs in the Central Area, ending its days in 1976 not far away at Plumstead Garage.

Below: RF594 (NF) was another to miss an Aldenham overhaul in 1968, and has terminated at Gravesend clocktower on route 450. Green Line routes 701, 702 and 725 also terminated here. Eleven years later, in the spring of 1979, the very last London RF of all in normal service would work in this area, as will be shown later.

By 27th April 1968, the New Town Services at Stevenage had expanded considerably, in line with the still-growing New Town. Routes 800 and 801 worked a 'frying-pan' shaped loop, running in both directions to the outer edges of the New Town from the Bus Station and then running together to the railway station, which was north of the Old Town. Here, RT597 (SV), as mentioned earlier originally the lowest-numbered postwar green RT, departs from the Bus Station, leaving two of its fellows behind. It is another to have a white fleetname, as applied experimentally in the summer of 1966.

On the same day, GS13 (HG) has just crossed the Great Northern Main Line north of Welwyn Garden City Station, having meandered its way through a number of scenic Hertfordshire villages on route 388 from Hertford. By now, only a dozen or so of these little Guy 26-seaters remained in service.

This picture, taken in Addlestone Garage on 9th May 1968, clearly shows the difference in height between an RT and an RLH. RLH45 and RT4783 are nearest the camera. Although both types were A.E.C. Regent IIIs, with the same engines, the RLHs also had standard A.E.C. radiators and wings - different from the RTs, too. With their sunken offside gangways and seats seating four people on the upper deck, they seated 53 people as opposed to 56 on an RT. In this view, RLH45 has lost its radiator badge. It is interesting that, thanks to the less rigid bus type-to-route allocations in the Country Area, both RTs and RLHs worked routes 420 and 461A at this time.

Above: Just along from Addlestone Garage, RLH50 (WY) awaits its crew during a changeover while working route 461 from Walton-On-Thames to Staines. The bus and coach stop flag, complete with red and green toggles on top to denote its dual function, is also of note.

Left: Whereas RLHs worked route 461 owing to low bridges on it, particularly the one in Chertsey Road, Staines, both RLHs and RTs worked route 461A. RT828 (WY) crosses the road junction by The Duke's Head pub in Addlestone heading for St. Peter's Hospital, Botleys Park. This RT is another ex-red RT3/1.

Waiting at the traffic lights at the same crossroads is RLH34 (WY) on its way from Guildford to Staines on the 436. It is actually a Guildford bus on loan to Addlestone and in this view, its wide upper-deck seats, for four passengers, and offside sunken gangway can be clearly seen. These buses looked much older than they really were, almost prewar, compared with the contemporary RTs.

RT3397 (LH), yet another green-ex-red RT3/1, passes through Epsom on 10th May 1968 on the very long trunk route 408, which ran all the way from Guildford to Chelsham, via Leatherhead, Epsom, Sutton and Croydon. Not only did much of this route skirt the edge of the Central Area, it also paralleled the 403 as far as Wallington from Chelsham and the 470 even further, to Leatherhead. The RT is in fact on loan from Chelsham to the latter garage and I had ridden on it from West Croydon to Epsom.

An RT on route 470, just visible on the left, took me to Dorking from Epsom. By now it is raining, and passengers have to brave the elements to board RF280 (RG) on route 439 in the bus station adjacent to the LT garage. This RF is one of several that were downgraded from Green Line coaches to Country buses on overhaul in the mid-1960s, though they retained their more comfortable coach seats. Two modernised Green Line RFs stand on the right; RF280 is now preserved in 1950s Green Line livery.

Back in the northern Country Area, it is a matter of opinion whether little GS33 (GR) on route 309 will have room for all the passengers waiting to board it in Rickmansworth High Street on the afternoon of 14th May 1968! If not, they could have travelled to Chorleywood on the Metropolitan Line! This GS is one of the many that survived into preservation.

Around the corner outside the station, RT3306 (GR), another ex-red RT3/1-bodied example, has terminated on a short working of the very long route 321. It stands amid roadworks altering the traffic layout at this location.

Green Line relief RT1021 (NF) arrives at Gravesend clocktower on 28th May 1968. Route 497 served Dover Road Schools, for where this RT will depart once it has turned around. It is another of the 'Green Line relief' RTs. Peculiarly, its front via blind-box has been masked.

A handful of GSs survived at Northfleet Garage at this period, though by now they were perhaps not really needed, since they worked on the same local routes as RFs, for instance the 450, 451, 489 and 490. On the stand at Gravesend cloctower, GS36 (NF) leads four RFs, one of which is a modernised Green Line example working route 701 all the way across London to Ascot.

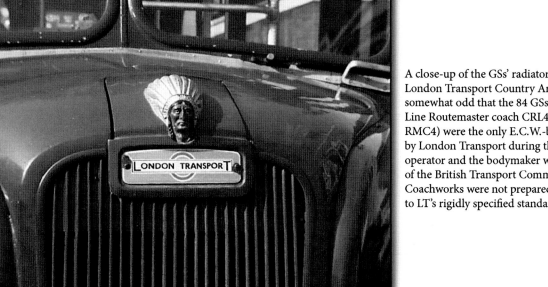

A close-up of the GSs' radiator badge, complete with London Transport Country Area emblem. It was somewhat odd that the 84 GSs, plus prototype Green Line Routemaster coach CRL4 (later renumbered RMC4) were the only E.C.W.-bodied vehicles bought by London Transport during the years when both the operator and the bodymaker were under the control of the British Transport Commission. Perhaps Eastern Coachworks were not prepared to produce bodies built to LT's rigidly specified standards?

The faded paintwork on RF673 (NF) running around the block at Gravesend terminus shows that this is another RF that missed overhaul in 1968. Despite that it remained in service until January 1976! Also, routes 489 and 490 would see the very last RF in normal public service, in the spring of 1979.

Right: The 1968 Derby was held the next day on 29th May, and one of several London Transport vehicles which have operated excursions to it is RCL2223 (RE). This sports the new Green Line livery first introduced on RMCs when they were overhauled during 1967/68; the RCL coaches were now three years old and undergoing inter-overhaul repaints.

Below: At Epsom Downs, RT3602 (LH) heads a line of buses on the special race service 406F to and from Epsom Station. Most are RTs, but the third one in the line-up is an RML from Godstone Garage. Buses from all over the Country Area, from as far a way as Luton and Stevenage, were loaned for the day for this busy service.

Sister RT3604 (LH) is another one of those adorned in Green Line livery in 1960s for relief duties. It accompanies a red RT at the terminus of route 93 at Epsom Clock Tower, working route 418. Interestingly, this Country Area route had some roads to itself well within the Central Area around Surbiton and Tolworth, and today survives as a London (red) bus route running from Kingston to Epsom, terminating at this spot! Meanwhile, somewhat oddly, although used mostly as ordinary Country buses by this time, most of these 'relief' Green Line RTs retained their coach livery, whereas those that had always been Green Line RTs which were replaced by RCLs in the East in 1965 were generally repainted into Country bus livery, and in fact many of them were overhauled as such during 1968.

On 1st June 1968, RML2414 (HH) is well-filled as it sets off from Uxbridge Station on the long 347 route to Hemel Hempstead. Most buses on this route were based at Garston Garage, the new RMLs having replaced RTs in the spring of 1966. However, this odd one was based at Hemel Hempstead (Two Waters) Garage.

The same occasion finds RT3251 (HE) turning into Belmont Road, Uxbridge on a short working of route 305A to Chalfont Common. This is a former Green Line RT that had been based at Romford, London Road for many years and although it still has a Green Line fleet name, it has gained external adverts and had its 'tween-decks raised bullseyes removed. It was overhauled in July 1968, gaining a much later body that had not been on a Green Line coach, then in September 1972 was one of 34 London Country RTs sold back to London Transport. It lasted until the very end of London RT operation at Barking in April 1979, and was subsequently preserved in red livery, now being part of the Ensignbus heritage fleet.

Further west on 1st June 1968, RT3259 (MA) passes through Slough town centre on the long route 353, which ran from Berkhamsted to Windsor. It too had originally been a Green Line coach, and was overhauled as a red bus in 1969.

Also in Slough Town Centre, RCL2258 (DG) still carries its original livery, though will soon be repainted, losing the light green stripes around its windows. It is working the last leg of the long 704, which ran from Tunbridge Wells to Windsor via Victoria.

As RCL2258 heads away in the distance, RMC1503 (DG) has passed it on sister route 705, which ran from Windsor to Sevenoaks. This is one of a handful working the two routes while the RCLs are undergoing their repaint cycle, and has itself recently been overhauled in the revised Green Line livery.

A number of Country Area RMLs worked in the Slough area, too. RML2446 (WR), whose registration number matches that of the route it is working, awaits departure from Slough Station on local route 446. This RML would have the distinction of being the very last in use in the former Country Area, and worked a farewell tour on 1st March 1980. One of the majority of London Country Routemasters bought back by London Transport, it spent 24 years working as a red bus, and is now preserved in that condition.

Southern peripheral Green Line route 725 ran all the way from Windsor to Gravesend, via Kingston and Croydon, but RF115 (ST) awaiting departure from Windsor Bus Station also on 1st June 1968 is 'only' going as far as Dartford! The splendid LT bullseye atop the waiting room which adjoins Windsor Bus Garage, along with the LT coach stop on the right all emphasise London Transport's corporate image, as established in the 1930s.

A number of Country Area bus routes operated specifically for visitors to various mental hospitals or isolation hospitals that were situated on the edge of the Greater London area. One was route 472, on which RT671 (LH) sets off from its home garage, Leatherhead, for Netherne Hospital on 5th June 1968. This was a limited stop service, and also had protected fares to ensure short-distance riders on sections of the route also served by ordinary Country bus routes did not crowd out those who needed to get to or from the hospital. The RT behind is a red one at the terminus of route 65; RT671 is yet another green-ex-red RT with an RT3/1 body.

Another of the class based at Leatherhead that skipped overhaul in 1967/68, a very well-filled RF621 (LH) passes The Running Horse pub in its hometown, working route 462.

Right: From Leatherhead, an RT on route 470 took me to Dorking, where RF199 (DS), another of the Green Line RFs downgraded to Country bus status in the mid-1960s, is nevertheless at work on Green Line coach route 714. It heads along the High Street; the Surrey Downs may just be glimpsed in the distance.

Below: Working scenic route 433 over the Downs, a solitary GS remained at Dorking Garage at this period. GS42 (DS) stands at Dorking North Station terminus. Four years later, this would be the last GS in service, on route 336A, and it too is now preserved.

Another RT on route 414 took me further out to Crawley, one of the southern extremities of the London Transport system. It was therefore another 'border town', served also by Southdown, one of whose single-deckers arrives at Crawley Bus Station as RT3125 (CY) awaits departure on route 426A. By sheer coincidence, this RT served as my 'wedding car' eight years later, having been preserved by a friend in 1973! It is now smartly restored to 1950s Country Area livery.

Route 438C linked Crawley with East Grinstead, another of LT's southern outposts. RT3053 (EG) departs from the Bus Station for its hometown, apparently devoid of passengers!

Inevitably, Crawley was also served by a number of routes operated by RFs. RF221 (CY), another former Green Line coach downgraded to bus status, loads up in the bus station on route 426, though it is unclear where it is heading since the driver has not changed its blind!

Aside from a solitary example at Victoria, Gillingham Street, the only production MB-types in service in June 1968, by which time more than 200 had already been delivered, were a small number in the Country Area. One of them is MB97 (RG), which stands at the Laker Hotel terminus of route 447 in Redhill. Union objections to what turned out to be really ghastly vehicles delayed their mass entry into service in the Central Area until 7th September, 1968. The Country Area was spared this 'privilege' even longer, until February 1969!

Returning to the northern Country Area, Tring was one of its smallest garages. On 29th June 1968, RF292 (TG), which is actually on loan from nearby Amersham Garage, has just run in on local route 387. As the brackets above its windows show, this was another that had been downgraded from a Green Line coach to a Country bus, but had originally been a red Central Area RF until converted to a coach in 1956!

Similarly, RF312 (MA) has also been downgraded from Green Line coach to Country bus status, but was a Country bus in the first place! As its registration number implies, it was also renumbered when converted to a coach in 1956 from RF531. This was done to keep all the Green Line coaches in one numerical block; RF292 was not renumbered since the red RFs so converted followed on numerically from the original Green Line batch. Many of the conversions numbered from RF289 - RF313 were based at Amersham Garage as this one is. It is standing at the terminus of local route 348A at Chesham Broadway.

Peculiarly, local route 442 at High Wycombe, at the north-western extremity of the Country Area, was numbered in the southern Country Area series, yet other local routes there, for example the 326 and 363, were in the northern one! Also on 29th June 1968, RF612 (HE) sets off from the small LT garage there for a trip around the town. Most local bus services here were operated by the Tilling Group subsidiary Thames Valley.

Saturday, 6th July 1968 was a busy market day in Dartford, where RT967 (DT) sets down passengers at the market place on route 423. Of note is the advert on its side for Green Rovers, which had just gone up from six shillings (30p) to seven shillings (35p) for the first time since early 1962! Red Rovers were the same price, and both were excellent value for money, covering the whole of the Country and Central Areas respectively: many of my travels on which the photographs in this book were taken were made possible using them. A Red Rover has taken me to Dartford on this occasion, as former trolleybus route 96 reached the town, as it still does today.

It was a busy market day at Hertford on Saturday 21st September 1968, too, as GS13 (HG) loads up in the adjacent Bus Station for the cross-country run on route 388 to Welwyn Garden City. A handful of GSs still worked from Hertford Garage at this time. The present shopping centre at Hertford, which the new bus station fronts, occupies the site both of this bus station and the car park on the left today.

The RT behind the GS in the previous picture is RT3675 (HF), which will pass its home garage at Hatfield on the way to St. Albans. It accompanies RF581 (HG) on route 308, which was also worked by GSs. Scenes like this typified the London Transport Country Area from the early 1950s, right through the 1960s and into the early years of London Country Bus Services Ltd.

Above: Much the same can be said of this scene in St. Albans, where it is also market day, a week later on 28th September 1968. Former Green Line RF216 (SA) terminates in St. Peter's Street, as RT4728 (GR) prepares to overtake it on the long trunk route 321 to Uxbridge. Six months or so later, this RT was replaced by MBSs on local routes in the Watford area, and overhauled as a red bus.

Right: Further out in the Country Area that day, relief Green Line RT620 (MA) approaches Amersham Station on route 362 which linked the Buckinghamshire towns of Chesham, Amersham and High Wycombe. A number of ex-Green Line RFs and RTs were based at Amersham Garage at this time.

Next day, 29th September 1968, Country bus RML2309 (WR) is a long way from home when working as a relief on Green Line route 718 at Harlow Bus Station. RMC-class Routemaster coaches were this route's normal allocation, from both Harlow and Windsor Garages at this time.

Above: Harlow's own RML2445 (HA) works a Sunday journey on route 397, displaying the 'Town Service' via blind usually used for routes 804 and 805, passing the Bus Station. Both of these RMLs passed to London Transport, with whom they saw more than twenty years further service, after withdrawal by London Country.

Left: On the same Sunday, RT3502 (GY) passes beneath the District and London Tilbury & Southend lines at Upminster Bridge Station on trunk route 370, linking Romford with Grays and Tilbury. This route still exists today as a London Buses service, though its eastern terminus is now the Lakeside shopping complex near Grays.

In Grays itself, RT2779 (GY) passes The Queens Hotel heading for Purfleet on route 371A. Whereas within a couple of years the 370 had converted to RMC operation, the 371 group of routes converted to RF. This trend continued in the early years of London Country operation, with RT-operated trunk routes gaining RMCs or RCL Routemaster coaches downgraded to bus status, and local routes converting to single-deck OMO using surplus RFs or new MBS and SM types. New OMO double-deckers began to replace them too in 1972, however RTs soldiered on working such routes as the 403 until 1976/77.

By late 1968, traditional Green Line coach routes were suffering loss of patronage due to the increase in private car ownership, which in turn aggravated traffic congestion that delayed them. Improved British Rail commuter services also had a detrimental effect on them. Route 717 was a typical victim. Running between Welwyn Garden City and Wrotham (its southern section having replaced route 703 earlier in the 1960s), it was withdrawn north of Baker Street at the end of December 1967, then completely just under a year later. Not long before its withdrawal, RF73 (SJ) heads through Foots Cray on its way to Wrotham on 27th October 1968. Route 719 was extended from Victoria to Wrotham to replace it.

The long 710, running from Crawley to Amersham, was another victim of all this, and was curtailed south of Baker Street. Shortly before this happened, RF186 (MA) passes County Hall (my place of employment at the time) on 21st November 1968. No direct replacement was made for the route's southern section, though routes 706, 707, 708 and 709 still covered the route between Kennington and Croydon. However, these too were further reduced early in 1969, as will be shown below.

RML2460 (WR) was the last double-decker built for London Transport's Country Area, also of course the last green one built for LT. It was approaching three years old when leaving Uxbridge Station for Windsor Castle on route 457A, which linked the two towns, on 19th January 1969. In common with most Country Routemasters, it passed back to London Transport after withdrawal, spending more than twenty years as a red bus. However, it suffered serious rear-end damage when rammed by another Routemaster and was withdrawn early. After languishing in a Yorkshire scrapyard for some years it was rescued for preservation, but is still undergoing rebuild as this book is compiled.

February 1969 saw not only the first major incursions of new MBS standee single-deckers in the Country Area, but also further cuts to the Green Line network, principally involving the Watford - Aylesbury and Victoria - Croydon 'corridors'. The 707, which ran from Oxted to Aylesbury, paralleling the 706 for much of its route, was withdrawn completely. On 6th February 1969, just over a week before its withdrawal, RF178 (TG) calls at Eccleston Bridge, Victoria. As is visible on its stop flag, routes 706 and 707 went to Aylesbury, whilst the 708 and 719 went to Hemel Hempstead. The latter, however, did so via a different route. It is also of note how this RF has a painted 'Please pay as you enter' sign below its nearside front window: these were just beginning to replace the orange plastic slipboards hitherto displayed in this position.

Route 708 had only received RMCs to replace its RFs at the end of 1967, these being displaced by the curtailment of the 717 and its reversion to RF operation. However their reign was very short-lived, since the 708 too reverted to RF working amid the cuts of February 1969. On 9th February 1969, a few days beforehand, RMC1505 (EG) calls at Buckingham Palace Road, Victoria, with very few passengers aboard. Southbound Green Line coaches had to stop here as a result of Eccleston Bridge being made one-way, northbound only, in the autumn of 1965. This RMC was one of two that went for scrap at the end of 1977, having been cannibalised for spare parts during the mid-1970s spares shortage.

Two very long Country Area trunk routes were the 303 and 303A, which somewhat ironically virtually paralleled the Great Northern main line between New Barnet and Hitchin. On 14th February 1969, their last day of full RT operation, RT3227 (HF) stands at their New Barnet Station terminus. This RT had originally been one of the Romford Green Line batch.

The RT shown above took me to Hatfield, where RT3156 (HF) calls at the former Great Northern railway station on local route 340A. The 340 group of routes converted to MBS OMO next day. Once again, this route served two stations on the G.N. main line as its rather sparse via blind shows.

Route 340B took a less direct route between New Barnet, Hatfield and Welwyn, and converted to MBS too. RT4172 (HF) heads along the Great North Road in Hatfield for its home garage also on the last day of RT operation. This RT was one of many that were overhauled in red after being displaced by Country Area route changes in February and March 1969 to replace roofbox RTs in the Central Area.

At Hatfield Garage itself, RT3375 (HF) has run in after the morning rush hour on local route 315, which will also be a victim of new MBSs next day. This RT was another ex-red one with an early RT3/1 body; it ended its days as a staff bus in the Central Area. Its stands outside the new Hatfield Garage opened in 1959, replacing the old one across the road. The use of a solid LT bullseye amid its name is interesting: the device in this form did not see general use in the Central Area until the 1970s.

Town services in Welwyn Garden City fell to the dreaded MBS next day, too. RT4515 (HF) stands outside the Great Northern railway station on Town Service 324 as new MBS404 passes by on type-training. This RT survived into London Country days and was one of the 34 sold back to London Transport in September 1972 to cover shortages of the type.

Across at St. Albans, local services were also converted to MBS OMO next day. However, route 313 was safe for now. Former Green Line RF229 (SA) departs from the small bus station in front of St. Albans Garage for Enfield. Route 313 became a London Buses (red) route in 1982, and still runs today linking Potters Bar, Enfield and Chingford. However, the splendid 1930s London Transport Country Area St. Albans Garage, whose offices form a backdrop to the RF, was the subject of a failed preservation project in the 1990s, and has subsequently been demolished.

RT3460 (SA) calls at St. Albans Garage on this very wintry day, on local route 354 whose odd blind arrangement shows the name Marshalswick three times! This was one of the routes that fell to the new MBSs next day, though in fact many were not brand new, having been in store since the previous summer. The splendid LT bus and coach stop on the right, complete with 'boat' beneath the stop flag advising passengers to queue either side of it depending on what route they wanted, is of note.

RFs at St. Albans did not escape from the encroachment of MBSs. They replaced them on route 391, on which RF652 (SA) passes the war memorial outside St. Peter's Church. In the event, many Country RFs outlived the MB-types, much as red ones did in the Central Area.

Hemel Hempstead local routes also succumbed to MBSs in February 1969. On its final day of RT operation, RT4111 (HH) approaches the Bus Station on route 314A. This was another RT to be overhauled in red as a result of these changes.

Watford local routes gained MBSs, too, which in some cases replaced RMLs. One group of routes involved was the 346 group, on which RT4125 loads up on an Oxhey Estate-bound 346 in Watford Market place in the final evening rush hour of official crew working. It also was overhauled as a red bus subsequently. Such was the abysmal service record of the MBSs that in the mid-1970s, RTs and RMLs returned to these routes, and red MB-types made redundant by London Transport had to be hired to help out, too!

Another area to receive new MBSs on local routes was Gravesend. One such was the 495, on which RT4121 (NF) heads away from Gravesend clocktower on route 495 bound for Christianfields Estate, complete with an upper-case via blind, on 5th March 1969, ten days before being replaced by MBS. This RT too was overhauled in red after being displaced.

RMLs, which were based at Northfleet Garage for the busy 480 between Erith and Gravesend worked local services there, too. RML2324 (NF) passes between The Sun (Truman's) and The Wheatsheaf (Charrington) pubs in Gravesend town centre in the evening rush-hour. This RML, as a red bus, would last until the very last day of normal Routemaster working in London in December 2005 - something that could never have been foreseen when I took this picture!

In total contrast to the new MBSs that would enter service at Northfleet Garage ten days later, GS54 (NF) runs out from the garage to take up service on route 490. It has just passed the Maidstone & District garage at Overcliff, outside which one of their Leyland Atlanteans stands. Two GSs remained in use at Northfleet until the autumn of 1969.

Yet another area to receive MBSs early in 1969 was Slough and Windsor, where they replaced RMLs which were only three years old on local routes. On 8th March 1969, a week before their introduction, RML2436 (WR) heads along Slough High Street on the 484. Although the RMLs, including this one, were redeployed onto other Country Area routes, this particular RML fell victim to the mid-1970s spares shortage and was one of seventeen that went for scrap at the end of 1977, when the rest of the fleet began to return to London Transport.

Captured from the window of a red RT heading in the other direction, RT1140 (SJ) draws into a stop on Orpington High Street on 5th April 1969, working route 477 skirting the Central Area between Dartford and Orpington, then continuing to the village of Chelsfield, which is actually within the London Borough of Bromley. Route 477 was one of the very last to use crew-operated vehicles (RMCs) for London Country, just lasting into 1980. The RT here is another RT3/1-bodied example that was originally red.

Route 486 was another Country Area route that worked well within the Central Area. Also on 5th April 1969, RF655 (DT), is packed to capacity when passing Bexleyheath clocktower on its way to Upper Belvedere.

On 3rd May 1969, Green Line relief RT610 (HA) turns into Station Road, Epping on its double-run through the town, which route 339 between Harlow and Brentwood did in both directions in order to serve Epping Station. Today, route 339 complete with RTs in Central Area, Country Area and Green Line livery, has been resurrected between Epping and Ongar to provide connections to the Epping Ongar heritage railway.

Right: A sunny Sunday 8th June 1969 finds RLH33 (GF) at the Staines, Moor Lane terminus of route 436. It appears to have lost its radiator badge. The RT behind is a red one on route 90.

Below: On the same day as the previous picture, RF74 (SA) calls at Heathrow Airport on the 727 Green Line Express. The route should have been operated by the troublesome RC class at this time, but inevitably RFs came to the rescue. This one is one of a number of Green Line examples modernised in 1966/67, but downgraded to bus status in 1968. That is why it has a 'London Transport' bullseye on the front and not a 'Green Line' one. The broad waistband on these vehicles was painted bright yellow, with the name 'London Transport' on the side in black lettering. Following London Country taking over in 1970, this livery was also adopted by them at first for their buses.

Inevitably, Green Line coaches occasionally broke down when in service, even despite the excellent reliability of RF, RM and RT types. An emergency Green Line coach was specially kept at both Gillingham Street (Victoria) and Riverside (Hammersmith) Garages, but on odd occasions this was not enough, particularly if a vehicle came to grief somewhere in the outer Central Area, a long way both from these two garages and Country Area ones. This has happened on the evening of 27th June 1969, when an RCL on route 705 has broken down, probably in the Bromley area. To come to the rescue, red RF405 (TB) has been summoned from the local garage and the stranded passengers transferred to it. It departs from Victoria, Eccleston Bridge, where the Green Line inspector has found a blind panel saying 'Windsor' to put in its windscreen. The RF, from route 227's allocation, is one of the last remaining crew-operated examples, without platform doors, but the 705 had a conductor anyway.

RC3 (SA) has actually made it to Luton on the 727 Green Line Express on 2nd July 1969, and stands outside the small LT Country Area garage in the town. Note the special LT coach stand flags, one at the front of the RC saying 'head stop', the other at the rear saying 'tail stop'. What price these in anyone's collection today?

One of the extremities of the London Transport Country Area, Luton was unique within the LT 'empire' in having its own Corporation bus fleet, which operated most local services in and around the town. Tilling Group operator United Counties also had a depot there, with services running to the north and west of the town. Most London Transport routes operated to the south and east into Hertfordshire, to such places as St. Albans and Hitchin. However an oddity was their route 360, which travelled out to the village of Caddington west of Luton, passing beneath the M1 motorway as it did so. Complete with its odd livery of light green waistband and white fleetnames, along with a lazy blind display, RT3081 (LS) arrives at its Luton terminus.

Routes 364 and 364A also travelled west of Luton; downgraded ex-Green Line RF69 reached as far as Whipsnade Zoo, to where it is heading through the centre of Luton also on 2nd July 1969.

Although some of the ex-red Country RTs with RT3/1 bodies that were due for withdrawal in 1968 actually were withdrawn, several others survived well into London Country days. One that did was RT4401 (RG), which passes through Purley Cross on the long 405 from West Croydon to Crawley on 13th July 1969. It was in fact one of three of these vehicles that were bought back by London Transport in September 1972, and quite remarkably it remained in service until 1978!

Another case of a red bus commandeered to rescue passengers from a broken-down Green Line vehicle, in this case an RMC, is that of RM611 (CF) on 18th July 1969. The RMC's front blinds for route 718 have been clumsily fitted to it as it speeds past Victoria Coach Station. This route passed through Camden Town, which is where the RMC probably came to grief, since the RM came from nearby Chalk Farm Garage.

Route 336A turned out to be the last outpost of GS operation. It ran between Rickmansworth Station, where GS17 (GR) accompanies an RF on the stand on 4th August 1969, and Loudwater Village. Narrow country lanes ran to the latter point, where the vehicle was outstationed. This arrangement came to an end in March 1972, when both the route and the last GSs (another one was kept as a spare) were withdrawn.

By 20th September 1969, local Orpington area route 471 has graduated from GS to RF operation. Downgraded ex-Green Line RF243 (DG) negotiates the turning circle at Orpington Station. The very small lettering on its blind would probably not please the 'disability lobby' today!

On the same day as the previous picture, Green Line relief RT1021 (NF) glints in the evening sun as it brings back spectators from the Biggin Hill Air Display on one of several extra journeys on route 410 operated for the event. It has just passed The Crown pub on Bromley Common.

Red RT2997 (SP) has been loaned to the Country Area for the 410 extras, too, and leaves Bromley North Station empty to return to Biggin Hill and carry more spectators homewards. This is almost certainly the last time a red RT ever worked this service, since the split between the Central and Country Areas took place just over three months later when the latter was taken over by the National Bus Company as their subsidiary London Country.

Above: Former Green Line RF306 (GY), which had originally been Country bus RF525 before conversion to a coach in 1956, loads up in Grays on route 371 on 25th October 1969. As mentioned earlier, the 371 group of routes had been converted from RT to RF OMO a few months previously. A number of Country Area routes were so treated in an effort to reduce operating costs and combat staff shortages; the process continued into London Country days. As may be seen, the RF still has the brackets above its windows where Green Line side route-boards were carried.

Above: Still in Green Line livery that drizzly day in Grays is RT3438 (GY), one of those so painted for relief duties in 1960, working local route 328. It was a longstanding practice that Green Line coaches did not carry external advertising, as obviously shown here.

Left: By now, service cuts to Green Line routes meant that some RMC class coaches were surplus to requirements, therefore they began to be used as buses, replacing RTs. At Tilbury Ferry also on 25th October 1969, RMC1466 (GY) has done so on route 370, but for now still carries Green Line livery. By the summer of 1972, all RMC and RCL coaches had been demoted to bus status, except for three of the latter kept for route 709.

Across the river, RF279 (NF), another downgraded ex-Green Line coach, arrives at a very wet Gravesend clocktower on local route 450. I chose this weekend, the last of British Summer Time of the 1960s and therefore the last 'summer' weekend that London Transport would operate Country bus and Green Line services, to travel throughout the Country Area on one of LT's Weekender tickets, which covered all LT services: my journey started on the Saturday by travelling to Upminster by Underground.

From Gravesend, I rode on an RML on route 480 to Dartford, from where I caught RT3154 (SJ) for a long ride through the rainy Kentish countryside on route 401 to Sevenoaks Bus Station. In this view, it awaits departure from the latter point to Belevedere Station. Today, the section of route 401 between Bexleyheath and Belvedere still exists as a red bus route, and continues to Thamesmead.

Also at Sevenoaks Bus Station, RF251 (DG) - yet another downgraded Green Line coach - splashes through the puddles on a very short working on route 402 back to its garage. The 402 was a longstanding trunk route that ran to Bromley North Station. It still had journeys that ran there until as recently as July 2017, when the last remnants of it were finally withdrawn.

An RT on route 403 took me from Sevenoaks to Chelsham Garage, where RF44 (CM) stands in fading light with one of its fellows at the terminus of route 706. It was then my means of travel back to Victoria, from where the Victoria Line took me straight home! By coincidence, the 706 would be the last Green Line route to have a full, official allocation of RFs, in 1973. Just visible in the background are some of the RTs which were stabled in the open yard of this small garage.

A shortage of RFs in the Country Area led to a number of spare red ones being loaned to it towards the end of 1969. On Sunday, 26th October 1969, the second day of my 'Weekender', my first port of call was Dorking, to where I travelled by RF on route 714 all the way from Kings Cross. At the garage, one of the red RFs, RF374 (DS) accompanies former Green Line RF239 in the yard. These red RFs remained in the Country area for some months after its takeover by NBC subsidiary London Country.

By now, the long route 414 had converted to OMO RF on Sundays. RF646 (RG) appears to only have a couple of passengers aboard, right at the back, when departing from Dorking Bus Station for West Croydon.

RF96 (GF), yet another downgraded Green Line coach, has taken me from Dorking on scenic route 425 to Guildford, where it awaits return to Dorking in the company of an Aldershot & District Dennis Loline. Of note is the sign on the bus shelter on the right saying that the 'L.T.E. 425' stops there. This term, 'London Transport Executive' had in fact ceased to exist on 1st January 1963, when management passed to the London Transport Board. However, a new L.T.E. came into being under Greater London Council control on 1st January 1970, but only embraced the Central Area (red) buses and the Underground.

Whereas route 408 was a very long one that ran from Guildford all the way to Chelsham, the 408A was a local route linking Guildford and Merrow. Curiously it was operated by both RTs and RLHs, despite there being no need for the latter to do so. In Guildford's second bus station in Onslow Street, the other side of the railway station, RT3116 (GF) awaits departure on this service, also in the company of an A&D Loline.

The two surviving RLHs of the 1950 batch were still going strong as London Transport's tenure of the Country Area services came to an end. Also at Onslow Street, RLH13 (GF) has arrived on route 463 from Walton-On-Thames. The single-decker behind it is in the fleet of Safeguard, an independent operator which ran local services in and around Guildford. Their livery was red and cream.

Illustrating the decline in patronage on traditional Green Line services, RF245 (ST) speeds through Turnham Green on 1st November 1969 working the 702 between Sunningdale and Gravesend apparently empty! For some reason, it is not carrying the side route-boards these coaches usually had.

The evening draws in as RT4490 (ST) heads along busy Staines High Street on local route 441C. This was a variation of route 441, which ran all the way from here to High Wycombe.

On a murky 23rd November 1969, RT3138 (GR) heads along the Oxford Road nearing its destination of Uxbridge Station on the long 321. Of particular note are the trolleybus traction standards, a relic of route 607 withdrawn more than nine years previously, in use for street lighting on the right, and the Uxbridge Odeon on the left. This RT was also one of the 34 that London Country sold back to London Transport in 1972, but it only ran as a red bus for a short time.

LONDON COUNTRY

London Country has been in existence for three weeks on 22nd January 1970, but so far nothing has changed vehicle-wise in the fleet, even down to RFs that had been working Green Line routes in the morning rush hour being switched to bus duties later in the day! In pouring rain at the Eardley Arms, Upper Belvedere, well within Central Area territory, modernised Green Line RF61 (DT) still carries its side route-boards for the 725 when working route 486 to Dartford.

Three weeks later, RT4531 (DT) is blinded for the same route when standing beside the offices at the entrance to Northfleet Garage on 15th February 1970. It has had its London Transport fleetname painted out, but still carries LT legal lettering and radiator badge.

Country bus RF557 (WR) has been pressed into service on route 725, on which it passes Kingston Station on Good Friday, 25th March 1970. Although it still has its London Transport fleetname, its front bullseye, which also housed the filler-cap on unmodified RFs, has been painted out spoiling its appearance somewhat. It has also gained new London Country legal lettering.

Similarly treated, RF681 (ST) proudly displays the new London Country fleetname, which was at first applied in non-underlined gold lettering. The panels accommodating it have been repainted, too. Working route 460 to Slough, it calls at a splendid old L.G.O.C. bus stop, complete with inspectors' telephone point, in Kingston Road, Staines.

At Staines, Moor Lane, terminus, RLH36 (WY) and RLH13 (GF) both also have the new fleetname, the latter very markedly so with two newly-painted side panels. Yet both still display London Transport adverts! RLHs would not last long with their new name and operator - all were withdrawn at the end of July 1970, replaced by new SM-class single-deckers.

Next day, 26th March 1970, RT3139 (HG) departs from Enfield Town on route 310A bound for Hoddesdon. Its LT radiator badge has gone, but it still bears LT fleetnames and front adverts for Green Rovers, though the offside one is torn! Sadly, the 310 and its derivations no longer run to Enfield today, terminating instead at Waltham Cross. Indeed, there are no 'cross-border' routes there at all now, with all red London bus routes also terminating there. A far cry from the good old days, when the 310 and 310A penetrated the Central Area as far as Enfield, and Central Area routes ran well beyond Waltham Cross into Essex and Hertfordshire on such routes as the 205/A, 217/A/B, 242/A and 279/A! Progress?

Two days later, on Easter Monday 28th March 1970, RT2982 (LH), another one of the ex-red RTs with RT3/1 bodies, changes crew outside Leatherhead Garage on its long journey on route 408 from Guildford to Chelsham. Once again, London Transport adverts are still carried, but its radiator badge has gone and the new London Country name applied.

At Orpington Station on 15th April 1970, RF277 (DG) awaits departure on route 431 for Sevenoaks, and still carries its full London Transport livery. The marks above its windows where the route-board brackets were may still be seen, several years after it was downgraded from a Green Line coach.

In Katherine Street, Croydon on 27th May 1970, RT3607 (RG) is at the start of its long journey to Horsham, via Redhill and Dorking. Of note is the advert on the side for Green Rovers, which though in the same style as the London Transport one, has now been revised to quote 'London Country bus routes' and show the new LCBS symbol, which soon gained the nickname 'The Flying Polo'.

In contrast, RML2310 (EG) which is working route 424, normally the preserve of the five remaining XFs and three recently acquired XAs at East Grinstead, where it loads up in the High Street, still displays London Transport adverts for Green Rovers. They are still 7/- (35p), as they had been since the summer of 1968. This RML was one of the first former London Country Routemasters to enter service in red after sale back to LT in early 1978.

Also in East Grinstead High Street, XA48 (EG) is one of three of this class, some of which had previously worked here in red livery for comparison with route 424's incumbent XFs, that were overhauled in Country Area livery late in 1969 to replace three XFs transferred to Stevenage Garage for the special 'Blue Arrow' service. To complicate matters, the three XAs were exchanged with three Country Area RMLs, duly painted red and sent to the Central Area immediately before the split-off of the Country Area from London Transport. Subsequently, when the remaining 47 XAs still with LT were sold to Hong Kong early in 1973, these three London Country ones joined them, and the three XFs at Stevenage returned to East Grinstead! Meanwhile, its somewhat odd that the XA here is working with a conductor, who may be seen standing next to the driver, complete with Gibson ticket machine.

Seemingly a more mundane vehicle, working local route 435 and passing East Grinstead Garage on the right, RF310 (EG) also has a complicated history. It began life as Country bus RF529 in 1953, but was converted to a Green Line coach in 1956 and renumbered RF310. Ten years later, it was downgraded to become a Country bus again, but not renumbered on that occasion!

A ride by RT on route 438C took me across to Crawley, where what would be my 'wedding car' just over six years later, RT3125 (CY) arrives at the bus station on local route 405B. It incorrectly has a side blind in its front via box, thus showing the route number twice.

One of the furthest areas away from Central London to the south that LT and London Country buses served was Horsham. Also on 27th May 1970, RT4765 (CY) arrives in the town on a short working of route 434, on which I had travelled there. Despite its balding roof, this RT survived long enough to be one of the 34 sold back to London Transport in September 1972, and saw another three years' service as a red bus, then two further years as a driver trainer with LT.

Also on a short working, this time of the 425, RF544 (DS) arrives at Dorking Bus Station, as I just had on an RT on route 414 from Horsham. The RF is actually on loan to Dorking from Guildford Garage, such loans being much more commonplace on Country Area and Green Line routes than they were in the Central Area.

An RF working the full distance on route 425 took me to Guildford, where RT3137 (GF) loads up on a short journey of local route 415 in Onslow Street Bus Station. Offside loading like this would never be allowed in today's Health & Safety era! Two Aldershot & District Dennis Lolines and an RLH complete the picture.

On the same occasion, RLH46 (GF) works a short journey on route 436 to the same destination as the RT seen above! The RT just visible on the left is operating the 415's full route through to Ripley. Time is now running out for the RLHs, which will be withdrawn just over two months later.

At Romford Market on 29th May 1970, RT4192 (GY) is still at work on route 370 despite the appearance of RMCs on this busy service. It still has its LT radiator badge and LT Green Rover adverts on the front, but the telephone number on the side one has been blanked out.

Passing beneath Bushey Arches on 6th June 1970, RT3002 (TG), a surviving ex-red RT3/1-bodied vehicle, is still in complete London Transport Country Area condition on its long journey on trunk route 301 to Aylesbury - except for London Country legal lettering!

In contrast, RT4489 (HH) sports a London Country fleetname but still has LT Green Rover adverts when passing the site of the former Watford High Street Garage. It is standing in for an RML on route 347, something that would become more common as the 1970s progressed owing to the worsening vehicle spare parts shortages.

On Sunday, 7th June 1970, RCL2237 (GD) crosses Oxford Circus on one of route 709's Sunday journeys from Godstone to Baker Street. This was one of just three RCLs that worked this route, running only during Monday to Friday rush hours and on Sundays. The driver wears one of the traditional LT white-topped caps dating from many years previously.

It is the last day of RLH operation in the former Country Area, Friday 29th July 1970, and RLH36 (WY) stands at the Ripley, Surrey terminus of route 436A bound for Staines. On the right, a 1930s London Transport timetable board may just be discerned. The RLH's London Country fleetname is only just visible, as if halfheartedly applied.

A lesser-known RLH working in their final years was that of route 420, which did not really need them and was also worked by RTs. RLH50 (WY) is caught at speed in Albert Drive, Sheerwater on its way to Woking Station on their final evening. The notice in the rearmost lower-deck window proclaims their replacement by new O.M.O. SMs next day.

After the evening rush hour, three RLHs have run in to Addlestone Garage for the last time, but RF666 (WY) runs out on route 456 for a trip to Woking. RFs would continue to operate from this garage for most of the ensuing decade.

A last look at a Country RLH: RLH14 (WY), one of the two survivors from the 1950 batch, has terminated at Walton-On-Thames and will work back to Addlestone Garage as a 461A on its very last run. A notice telling of the replacement of these antiquated-looking vehicles by O.M.O. SMs next day is visible on the window behind the driver's cab, facing into the lower saloon.

Green Rovers have been increased to 8/- (40p), but although the adverts for them has been altered to show the new price, they still display the LT symbol on RT970 (HA) standing at Epping Station on 5th September 1970.

Right: The same phenomenon is displayed on the nearside advert on RT671 (GF), though the offside one has a London Country symbol! It passes Carshalton Ponds on the 408's long journey from Chelsham to Guildford on 25th September 1970.

Below: Routes 406 and 406A were also converted to RF OMO on Sundays at this period. On 18th October 1970, RF586 (RG) sets off from Kingston Southern Region Station for Redhill on the latter route. Behind it, a Bulleid-designed 4SUB EMU has also terminated there.

A light dusting of snow is evident as RF683 (WR) stands at the Uxbridge Station terminus of route 459 on 28th December 1970. London Transport's new Uxbridge Garage was built on this site in the mid-1980s, and is still in use as this book is compiled.

At the start of route 310's journey to Hertford, in Church Street, Enfield Town, RT4767 (HG) has just been overhauled and repainted in the new London Country livery of Lincoln Green, with yellow waistband, stocknumber and fleetname, plus a 'Flying Polo' emblem behind the rearmost offside lower-deck window. The date is 29th May 1971. Despite now being a separate entity, London Country's buses were still overhauled at Aldenham at this period, though sadly this smart new livery would only be applied for a couple of years. However, those Country RTs that were overhauled at Aldenham in 1971/72 did not change bodies. The last was done in April 1972, bearing a lighter green livery than hitherto used.

RT4752 (SJ) has also gained the London Country emblem, though not been overhauled as the nasty dent by the driver's cab door shows. It sets off on Whit Monday, 31st May 1971 from Bexley Mental Hospital on one of route 401's special journeys there.

Even after London Country became a separate entity, red London Transport buses still on rare occasions stood in for broken down Green Line coaches. On 17th July 1971, RM428 (HT) from Highgate Garage has come to the rescue of a RMC that must have come to grief somewhere in the FinsburyPark or Holloway area on route 715. Complete with a clearly chalked number and destination, and an 'On hire to London Country Bus Services Ltd' sticker in its front lower-deck window, it passes Shepherd's Bush Green on its way to Guildford.

Although some Country RTs were being overhauled in 1971, mass withdrawals of standard examples were now under way as a result of their replacement by new SMs. RT1097 and RT3191 are nearest the camera in this view of a number of them awaiting disposal in the yard of Grays Garage on 11th August 1971. Sadly, in common with their red counterparts, most made a one-way journey to the Yorkshire scrapyards.

Far more dead RTs were at Grays at this time than those allocated there for service, one of which, RT3675 (GY) appears to be abandoned in the middle of nowhere! It is in fact standing at the Stifford Clays terminus of route 328.

Right: Stevenage Garage's large fleet of RTs were still going strong on most of the New Town routes on 29th August 1971. RT3461 (SV) negotiates a Bailey bridge in Six Hills Way on circular route 801. This RT would be one of three to operate in National Bus Company corporate light green livery six years later, and was later preserved in that condition.

Below: In complete contrast, and at the same location, brand new Metro-Scania MS1 (SV) is working the new Superbus service which had recently replaced RT-operated route 809, adorned in a smart blue and yellow livery. All told, seven of these vehicles worked the Superbus services, alongside SMs and LN-class Leyland Nationals, but all had been withdrawn by the end of the 1970s. Chells was a somewhat remote part of the New Town at this period.

Above: Chells was also served by the Blue Arrow commuter services, for which XF6, 7 and 8 had been allocated to Stevenage late in December 1969 and painted in a light blue and silver livery. XF8 (SV) accompanies an RF outside Stevenage Garage. After overhaul in 1972, they returned to East Grinstead.

Left: The days of RMC1466 (GY), which gleams in the winter sunshine as it heads out of Barking town centre on the 723 on 28th December 1971, as a Green Line coach are numbered. The route will be converted to RC operation just three days later. Within six months, all RMCs and RCLs except the three at Godstone on route 709 will be demoted to bus status, and used to replace RTs.

The same goes for RCL2234 (GY) on the 723A, just around the corner in East Street, Barking. This route was actually withdrawn just three days later, and replaced by a few extra journeys on the 723! The ill-fated RCs would fare no better on this route that elsewhere, and often had to be substituted by RMCs and RCLs, now officially downgraded to bus status, and even elderly RFs!

The RCLs on the other principal Green Line route serving Aldgate were replaced at the end of 1971, too. Also on 28th December that year, RCL2227 (RE) heads out of Romford with a good load of passengers aboard heading into London. The new RP class of Park Royal-bodied A.E.C. Reliances replaced them, sadly faring little better than the similar RCs. This RCL was one of two that expired during the vehicle spares shortage of the mid-1970s, and was scrapped early in 1978. Otherwise, most of the class had replaced RTs on trunk routes 405 and 414 in the southern London Country area, and all but one of them returned to London Transport, eventually being overhauled as red buses in 1980. The exception was RCL2221, which LT used as a mobile exhibition for the LT Museum.

A visit to Stevenage on Easter Sunday, 2nd April 1972, finds RT4176 (SV) at the railway station ready to set off for New Town circular route 800. This station on the Great Northern main line was located north of the Old Town, a long way from the New Town built south of it. Despite the fact that the New Town centre and bus station were situated close to the main line, and established from 1947 onwards, the railway station was not relocated there until the summer of 1973! That's 'town planning' for you!

Although the main trunk route 303 had lost RTs in February 1969, and by now was operated by the awful MB-types, Sunday journeys were operated on it using RTs between Stevenage and Hitchin for the benefit of hospital visitors. Accompanied by another RT on route 800, RT3134 (SV) awaits departure from the Bus Station. These journeys remained even after Stevenage lost most of its RT allocation when the New Town services converted to AN O.M.O. in October 1972.

Illustrating the recent demotion of RMC-class Green Line coaches to bus status, RMC1483 (DT) has terminated at Dartford Garage on Easter Monday, 3rd April 1972, on formerly RT-operated route 423. However, this route in turn would soon gain the underpowered and therefore unsuccessful SM-type, two of which stand in the garage yard.

Accompanying the RMC at Dartford is RT4047 (SJ) awaiting the off on route 477. This route converted to RMC operation soon afterwards and would retain them until early 1980, being one of the last London Country routes to retain Routemasters. Of note are the two trolleybus traction standards, visible above and behind the RT, used to illuminate the garage yard. They are relics of trolleybus route 696 which terminated not far away at Dartford Market Place and was replaced by bus route 96 in March 1959.

A packed Country bus RF584 (SJ) approaches Swanley Garage on Green Line route 719, heading for Wrotham. The reason it is so busy is that many of the passengers are heading for Brands Hatch motor racing circuit, where there is the usual Easter Monday race meeting.

Outside Swanley Garage, the RF has caught up RT3145 (SJ) working a Relief journey on the 719. One of those recently overhauled, the RT is in fact terminating at Brands Hatch, despite showing the destination 'West Kingsdown'. Of note is the 1930's London Transport timetable display case to the right of the RT.

Most buses at Chelsham Garage were kept in the yard, as the garage itself was very small and only usually used for vehicle maintenance. This view, also on Easter Monday 3rd April 1972, illustrates the transition London Country's vehicles were going through at the time. RTs dominate, of which RT3175 and RT4763 (CM) stand here, though newer buses such as SM511 on the left have been replacing them over the past two years of so. On the right, RF254 has come to grief in a nasty accident, and therefore been withdrawn - though the withdrawal of these reliable single-deckers, now twenty or more years old, is proceeding anyway.

Looking very sorry for itself, minus engine and cab, withdrawn RT1563 stands in a field at the back of Chelsham Garage and is in use as a uniform store. Surely, the uniforms would have got damp in this exposed location? Yet the RT fulfilled this role for several years there!

At Victoria, Buckingham Palace Road, the same evening, RCL2225 (DG), newly demoted to bus status, is working a Green Line relief on route 705, which had lost these vehicles only a few days before. However this one had been at Romford, London Road on route 721, and was the other of the two scrapped early in 1978.

A remarkably long Country route which survived well into London Country days was the 350A, which ran all the way from Bishops Stortford to New Barnet, via Hertford and Potters Bar. On 15th April 1972, RF559 (HG) descends Barnet Hill near the end of its long journey. Note the reduced blind display, needed because Hertford Garage operated so many different RF routes at this period, brief details of whose via and destination points all had to be accommodated on one blind!

Presumably by coincidence, routes 715 and 715A which had been the first Green Line routes to operate production RMCs in August 1962, were also the last to have a full allocation of them. On 21st April 1972, a couple of days before they were replaced by new RPs, RMC1484 (GF) turns from New Cavendish Street into Portland Place bound for Guildford on the 715. The Post Office Tower forms an interesting backdrop.

On 27th May 1972, RT4722 (LH) runs home to Leatherhead Garage when descending Sanderstead Hill. Three weeks later, route 470 and the associated 408 converted to AN O.M.O. This RT was one of the 34 sold back to London Transport in September 1972, but unlike many of the others, lasted only a short time as a red bus.

Next day, Sunday, 28th May 1972, RT597 (SV), numerically the first postwar Country RT, deposits a lone passenger in a section of Valley Way, Stevenage, that at this time was served only by special limited stop Hospital route 808, which ran from Hitchin to Chells in Stevenage New Town. The flag on the bus stop points this out. Unfortunately, having a canopy blind wrongly inserted in the front number blind box makes the RT appear as it is uncertain whether it is working route 303 or route 808 - it should be showing the latter!

On the last day of RT operation on routes 408 and 470, Friday 16th June 1972, RT4494(LH) passes through Wallington Green bound for Chelsham. It still looks smart, but has not been overhauled since May 1966, and will be withdrawn in July 1972. It was, however, subsequently preserved.

Left: On 12th July 1972, RF614 (GR) stands at the Croxley Green Station terminus of route 318. Interestingly, the destination states 'Croxley L.M.R. Station', to distinguish it from Croxley Metropolitan Line Station that the route also served. At the time this book is compiled, it is still unclear whether the long-proposed diversion of the Metropolitan Line in Watford, to link the two stations and proceed along the presently closed Croxley Green branch to Watford Junction will actually happen.

Below: Next day, 13th July 1972, RT4113 (GR) awaits its crew in Bushey Mill Lane, Garston on local route 385. Two days later, the associated 385A and trunk route 321 will convert from RT to AN O.M.O. This RT was withdrawn as a result, but sold back to London Transport in September.

Having taken me from Garston to Luton on trunk route 321, RT3135 (GR) sets off from Park Square on its return journey to Rickmansworth. This RT was also withdrawn as a result of replacement by the new ANs, but went for scrap two months later.

Also in Luton that day, RF94 (SA), one of the modernised Green Line RFs downgraded to bus status, loads up on route 365, which travelled to St. Albans via Wheathampstead, rather than the direct route the 321 took via Harpenden. A United Counties Bristol Lodekka just noses in behind it.

Another RF has taken me from Luton to Hitchin, where similarly downgraded modernised RF34 (SA), awaits departure at St. Mary's Square on route 304 to St. Albans. This route did not also serve Luton and travelled there via Whitwell. An RP which had replaced RMCs on the 716 in March, and an MB on the 303 stand behind it. Oddly, no fewer than four LT 'dolly' stops are in use here on this occasion.

Above: My next port of call was Stevenage, where RT3752 (SV) departs from the bus station bound for Chells, the driver having forgotten to change his blind. In April 1972, this was the last Country RT to be overhauled, and was outshopped in a lighter shade of green. This shade was subsequently used on other vehicles, notably RMLs, until supplanted by NBC corporate light green livery in 1973/74. RT3752 had been transferred here from Leatherhead Garage upon the AN conversion of the 408 and 470 four weeks previously, and would move back south in October, to Chelsham, when most of Stevenage's RTs were also replaced by ANs.

Left: Stevenage RTs operated an intricate set of Town Service routes during rush hours to and from the Industrial Area, which was the other side of the track of the Great Northern main line from the New Town itself. RT3134 (SV) heads along Gunnels Wood Road in this area on route 802B, as an SM on one of the recently-introduced 'Superbus' routes goes in the other direction.

Above: First overhauls of Country RMLs began at Aldenham in January 1972, albeit without bodychange. For some reason, RML2319 (GD) was only given a recertification, in May 1972, and on 14th July that year awaits return to Godstone Garage in West Croydon Bus Station. At the end of 1973, it was delicensed, and was never to run again, falling victim to the vehicle spares shortage of the mid-1970s and being cannibalised to keep others in service. It was one of seventeen Country RMLs that went for scrap early in 1978.

Right: In its new role as a Country Area bus, RCL2235 (RG) also awaits departure from West Croydon Bus Station on route 405 for Crawley. This bus station, which originally opened in 1964, has been rebuilt twice since this picture was taken. Thankfully, the monstrous office block behind it has been demolished, too!

On the same day, RMC1488 (SJ) also fulfils its new role as a Country bus when approaching Orpington Station on route 477. An RF on route 431 heads away in the opposite direction. Both this RMC and the RCL above are adorned with external advertising, which they never had when operating as Green Line coaches.

Top: Flanked by two red RFs which had replaced RTs on a number of routes at Uxbridge Garage in January 1971, RF173 (MA) pulls off the stand at Uxbridge Station to work a journey on the much truncated Green Line route 710, which now only ran from this point to Amersham. This was a far cry from when it ran all the way through Central London to Crawley, and soon even this remnant would be withdrawn.

Centre: Something of an oddity were the Express journeys that ran on route 403 between West Croydon and Warlingham in rush hours, especially since the route retained RTs until almost the end of crew operation with London Country. On 30th August 1972, RT4549 (CM) heads along Sussex Road, South Croydon along which this route ran rather than the Brighton Road which it paralleled. Note the 'Minimum Fare 5p' slipboard beneath its canopy. This was a 'protective fare' aimed at restricting these Express journeys to longer-distance riders. The normal minimum fare was all of 3p at the time!

Bottom: Subsidences in Lee High Road during 1972/73 caused disruption to several bus services in the area, with southbound journeys having to be diverted along Brandram Road, a residential street. This caused outrage to residents, who also had to put up with Green Line route 719 passing their doors! Also on 30th August 1972, RF144 (SJ) heads along it bound for Wrotham, and is oddly missing the 'Flying Polo' symbol on its front. This view clearly shows the filler cap, which had formed part of the raised LT bullseye originally fitted to RFs.

In contrast to the RF shown previously, RF41 (DG) is a former Green Line coach that had been downgraded to bus status in the mid-1970s. On 3rd October 1972, it passes through Bromley Market place on the 402's long run to Sevenoaks, and has recently been repainted into London Country's new livery of Lincoln green with yellow fleetname and stocknumber. Note also the reduced blind display, needed owing to the number of different routes RFs worked from Dunton Green garage, in similar fashion to those at Hertford.

In Aldenham Works being overhauled on 4th October 1972, XF7 (SV) still carries the Blue Arrow livery in which it, along with XF6 and XF8, had been painted late in 1969 for this new service at Stevenage. Alongside it is XF3 (EG) also under overhaul. In the event, all eight XFs returned to East Grinstead, their original home on route 424, after overhaul. The three XAs that had replaced them there were withdrawn and sold to Hong Kong, and the Blue Arrow service at Stevenage was replaced by extra 'Superbus' services.

Autumn leaves fall around modernised but downgraded Green Line RF169 (HA) which has arrived at Welwyn Garden City Station on cross-country route 393, which ran from Harlow via Hertford, on 5th October 1972.

On the evening of the same day, former Green Line RT3247 (SV) stands at the Bandley Hill, The Fold, terminus of Industrial Area route 802, whose destination blind reads 'Bandley Hill via White Lion, Industrial Area'. Bandley Hill was originally on the outskirts of Stevenage New Town, but in later years the New Town grew well beyond it! A week after this picture was taken, RTs ran on the Stevenage New Town routes for the last time, being replaced by new O.M.O. ANs next day.

Modernised Green Line RF165(SV) calls at the New Lister Hospital, just north of Stevenage, while working one of the hospital journeys of route 303 between Hitchin and Stevenage on a wet, gloomy Sunday 10th December 1972. These journeys were hitherto RT-operated, and peculiarly this RF has a conductor on board!

A week later, on 17th December 1972, RP27 (SV), one of the ninety Park Royal-bodied A.E.C. Reliances which replaced RMCs and RCLs on Green Line coach routes earlier in the year, also calls at The New Lister Hospital, but going in the opposite direction on the 716's long trek from Chertsey. Although the 303 and 716 paralleled each other between Hitchin and Stevenage, the coach of course did not observe all stops, whereas the bus did.

Right: Hospital route 808 was still running at this time, but now converted to O.M.O. RF. Apparently with no passengers aboard, RF597 (SV) negotiates Coreys Mill Roundabout on the old Great North Road between Hitchin and Stevenage.

Below: By this time, the 'Superbus' services in Stevenage New Town had become well-established. Bearing a special blue and yellow livery, SM496 (SV) departs from Stevenage Bus Station leaving one of its fellows behind. Sadly, these buses were just as troublesome with London Country as they were with London Transport, and all had perished by the spring of 1981.

1973 was the year in which London Country's Green Line RFs were retired from their original duties some 22 years after their original introduction - officially at least! On 23rd February 1973, RF93 (HE) passes The Grapes pub in Sutton High Street, on the 711's long journey from Reigate to High Wycombe. It is noticeably bereft of passengers, once again reflecting the decline in Green Line's fortunes. The use of Leyland Nationals with horrible plastic seats to replace the RFs did not improve matters!

Above: Back at Stevenage, on 18th March 1973, AN5 (SV) represents the Park Royal-bodied Leyland Atlanteans that replaced most of the RTs on the New Town services. It stands at the old G.N.R. railway station, now soon to be replaced by the new one, and already has some nasty dents on its offside skirting panels, despite only having been in service for eleven months, initially working route 310 at Hertford. These buses were painted in 'mid-green' and bright yellow and perpetuated the London Transport tradition of a three-piece front blind display.

Below: During the spring of 1973, Ponsbourne Tunnel on the Great Northern Hertford Loop had to be rebuilt to allow for the overhead electrification of the line, entailing its closure between Cuffley and Hertford. Several spare London Country RTs were drafted in to Hertford Garage to operate a railway replacement service, running through country lanes normally only served by RFs on route 308. On 21st March 1973, RT4550 (HG) stands beside a splendid British Railways Eastern Region sign at Cuffley Station.

Prior to the formation of London Country, red buses (latterly RTWs) were based in the Country Area as driver trainers. After the split with London Transport, Country RTs took over these duties. On 28th March 1973, RT1043 (RG) passes Stockwell Station heading for downtown Brixton.

By 19th April 1973, the vehicle spare parts shortage that affected both London Transport and London Country was beginning to bite. Country Routemasters were particularly badly affected and it was fortunate there were plenty of spare RTs to cover for them. RT3450 (GD) has been allocated to Godstone Garage, which lost its RTs when RMLs replaced them on routes 409, 410 and 411 in the autumn of 1965, for this purpose, and passes along South End, Croydon, on its way to Forest Row, one of the most distant points in the southern Country Area from Central London.

Easter Monday, 23rd April 1973, ended up very wet! RML2457 (WR) arrives at Victoria, Buckingham Palace Road, bringing day trippers homewards from Windsor, working a Green Line relief. It has recently been overhauled in London Country's new National Bus Company corporate livery of light green and grey waistband.

On 26th April 1973, RF613 (HG) arrives at Hertford Bus Station newly repainted in NBC corporate livery. With their front bullseyes painted out and the fleet name above the windows, as well as having no relief piping around the windows, RFs in this livery looked completely blank!

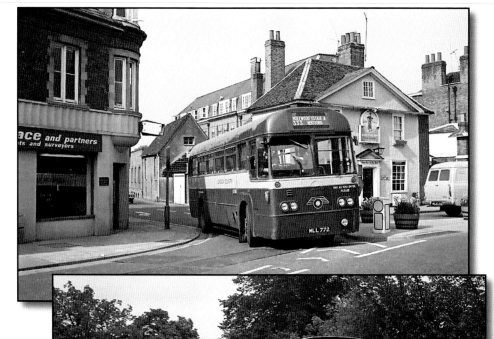

One of plenty of RFs working in Hertford that day, downgraded modernised ex-Green Line RF235 (HG) passes The Blue Coat Boy pub in the centre of town working local route 333, which had been one of the haunts of GSs. This would be the last year that RFs dominated the scene here - a combination of route cuts and replacement by new Bristol single-deckers of the BL and BN classes soon decimated them.

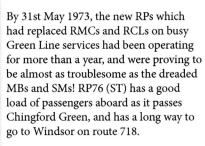

By 31st May 1973, the new RPs which had replaced RMCs and RCLs on busy Green Line services had been operating for more than a year, and were proving to be almost as troublesome as the dreaded MBs and SMs! RP76 (ST) has a good load of passengers aboard as it passes Chingford Green, and has a long way to go to Windsor on route 718.

In contrast to the new RPs, and even more so the similar RCs, RFs that were between twenty and twenty-two years old were still going strong, and often called upon to replace such newer types. On 2nd June 1973, modernised former Green Line RF103 (GY) has recently been repainted in an odd livery of light green with yellow waistband, and is covering for one of the unhappy RCs on route 723, passing through Canning Town. Of note is the former trolleybus traction standard behind it, one of several in this area retained as street lighting columns.

An RC that actually has managed to keep going on the 723 is RC4 (GY), which collects passengers at Rainham War Memorial on the same day. The similarity in appearance to the newer RPs is of note; this basic body design having originated with B.E.T. Group fleets following the introduction of 36ft-long buses and coaches in the early 1960s. Three red buses may be glimpsed in the background - an RML on route 165, an RT on route 87 and an SMS on route 103.

Adorned in the new N.B.C. corporate livery, RML2438 (GR) has only been recertified and not overhauled following its seventh 'birthday'. It passes through Borehamwood's industrial area on a short working of route 306 to the town on 5th June 1973. In October 1974, it will fall victim to the vehicle spare parts shortage and never run again, being scrapped in January 1978.

Next day, 6th June 1973, was Derby Day, on which RMC1462 (LH) is stuck in race traffic at Tattenham Corner. This important trunk route had by now been converted to RMC operation, but RTs persisted on it as late as 1978. A couple of typical 1960s/early 1970s coaches bringing spectators to the races may be observed on the left.

1973 was the last year that RTs dominated the special route 406F racegoers' service between Epsom Station and Epsom Downs. They provided almost the entire service, except for a couple of RMCs, RCLs and RFs. RT4747 (RG) is overheating as it arrives at Epsom Downs, a common problem with RTs in their later years. Luckily, and inspector was on hand with a watering can!
The scores of cars on the right illustrate how more and more people were travelling by car to the races by now, eventually rendering the buses redundant.

Recently-overhauled RML2453 (ST) crosses Staines Bridge on local route 441C on 19th June 1973. Not yet being fitted with external advertising does not enhance its appearance in the drab, corporate N.B.C. livery. Unlike some of the other RMLs illustrated herein, this one passed back to London Transport and remained in service until July 2005.

Some of the RMLs at Staines Garage were also by now falling by the wayside as a result of the vehicle spare parts shortage. A number of RTs were drafted in to cover for them, one of which, RT4046 (ST), heads along Church Street, Staines on an evening rush hour journey on route 469 - at the time more usually operated by RFs. The use of an RML's side blind in the via box predates this arrangement some six months later, when it was used on RTs allocated as spares for defunct RMs in the former Central Area.

Following a trend established a couple of years beforehand by London Transport, a number of London Country vehicles were adorned in all-over advertisement liveries in the early 1970s. On 18th August 1973, AN34 (GF) awaits the off at West Croydon Bus Station. Somewhat perversely, its adverts for Typhoo Tea had a basic red livery! Unlike their counterparts with London Transport, the dreadful DMSs, London Country's AN-class Leyland Atlanteans operated successfully for as long as twenty years or so, some of the type even being purchased secondhand in the fleet's latter years.

On the same day, RML2314 (GD) calls at Caterham Station, terminus of the commuter branch off the Brighton main line at Purley, prior to its arduous climb up Caterham Hill on the way to West Croydon on trunk route 409. This RML had been overhauled early in 1972 in traditional Country Area livery, which it retained until withdrawal in the late 1970s. It too passed back to LT and remained in service until July 2005. Also of note in this picture is the Southern Electric sign above the station entrance, still there more than 25 years after nationalisation!

On 13th January 1974, 'short' Leyland National SNC78 (RE) stands at Aldgate Minories Bus & Coach Station prior to setting off for Brentwood. These N.B.C. standard vehicles, painted in all-over green and without even a fleet name, have replaced RPs on the 721 and, in effect, finally killed this once busy Green Line route off. One of the main complaints about them was their uncomfortable plastic seats. However Leyland Nationals were at least more reliable that the MBs and SMs which they were now replacing, as well as older ex-LT types.

As if symbolising the problems London Country's Routemasters were now having with the spares shortage, RT1044 (HH) stands in for an RML on route 347, which had received the type eight years before this picture of it crossing the Great Central and Metropolitan Lines at Northwood Station was taken on 30th March 1974.

Illustrating the type of vehicle that was used to replace the remaining RFs on Green Line services in 1973, SNC78 (GR) loads up at Eccleston Bridge, Victoria on Easter Monday, 15th April 1974. It is a standard Leyland National bus, despite being classed as a 'coach'. Such vehicles were also used to replace RFs, RTs and Routemasters on bus services throughout the London Country fleet. Although they were a successful design, they were not appreciated by Green Line passengers, having bus-type plastic seats, as mentioned earlier. Their all-green livery didn't help, either, though subsequently they were painted green and white in standard N.B.C. 'dual-purpose' fashion. The RF behind the Leyland National is RF145 (EG) working route 708, probably duplicating one of the scheduled Nationals which had replaced RFs on this route some months previously. The 708 travelled by a more direct route to Hemel Hempstead than the 719, and this RF doubtless gave a more comfortable ride than the National on that route, too!

An odd class of vehicle delivered to London Country early in 1972 were the SMAs. These were Alexander-bodied A.E.C. Swifts that formed a diverted order from South Wales Transport. There were twenty-one of them in all, all but one of which were initially used on southern peripheral Green Line route 725. Like their bus counterparts, the SMs, they proved to be underpowered, and all were withdrawn by the end of 1981. On 15th April 1974, SMA10 (NF) is on loan to Windsor Garage, and also finds itself at Eccleston Bridge, working route 705.

London Country was still operating special routes serving hospitals on the outskirts of London in the spring of 1974. On 29th May that year, RT4102 (GR) approaches Bushey & Oxhey Station on limited stop route 345 to Napsbury Hospital. It wrongly has a side blind in its front via box.

On the same day, RML2439 (GR) heads along a remarkably traffic-free Watford High Street on local route 311 bound for Shenley. It was one of a number of RMLs in the second batch of CountryArea examples (RML2411-2460) which were only given recertifications in 1972/73 rather than full overhauls, though this one did survive to be bought back by London Transport at the beginning of 1978.

Right: Also in Watford that day, RF177 (CM) stands in for an SNC on route 706 as it passes a new National bearing the green and white Green Line livery in Water Lane. It is working the 706's seasonal extension to Chartwell, former home of Sir Winston Churchill.

Below: Collecting passengers in Watford Parade, RF610 (WR) has a nasty dent to its front dome on the nearside as it works route 335, hitherto an RT-operated route which ran all the way from Watford to Windsor, via Staines and was now theoretically MB-operated. An annoying trend at this time was for RFs to be plastered with adverts where their fleetnames should be, though at least the one on this RF, which is in a lighter shade of green than usual, does advertise for busmen!

Below: Perhaps one of the most inane all-over advertisements to appear on any London Transport or London Country vehicle during the fad for them in the early 1970s was that for Wimpy Bars. It was meant to resemble a burger, being painted in a glaring orange, yellow and white! The unfortunate recipient was Green Line coach RP46 (SV), which is passing Monks Wood, Stevenage bound for distant Chertsey on 30th May 1974.

Illustrating the new green and white N.B.C. 'dual purpose' livery now being given to RPs and SNCs, RP19 (SV) is on training duties when also passing Monks Wood that day.

Another all-over advertisement vehicle operating in Stevenage that day is Atlantean AN7 (SV) promoting 'Colour TV by Rediffusion', in a basic light blue livery. It heads out of the New Town centre on Town Service 813.

Back in Watford, RML2427 (GR) illustrates how virtually any type of vehicle could appear on any route in the London Country system at this period, as it heads for Abbots Langley on route 318 with an AN on the 385 following. They are crossing the West Coast main line just north of Watford Junction station on 4th June 1974. Despite being smartly adorned in corporate NBC livery, this RML was another only to be recertified rather than overhauled, and succumbed to the vehicle spare parts shortage in March 1975, never to run again.

With a somewhat confusing blind display, RF155 (HH) pulls away from the stop in Beechen Grove, Watford bound for Hemel Hempstead. It is one of the by now many modernised Green Line RFs that have been downgraded to bus status.

By the summer of 1974, London Transport had given up the ghost with the awful MB-types and was replacing most of them by the equally frightful DMSs. This did London Country a favour to some extent, in that many redundant MBs still had certificates of fitness, therefore they hired several of them from LT in an effort to help with their own problems caused by the ongoing shortage of spare parts. On 5th June 1974, red MB124 (LH) loads up on route 468 in Epsom High Street as an AN on the 408 brings up the rear. An 'On hire to London Country' sticker may just be discerned in the MB's nearside front window.

5th June 1974 was also Derby Day, and most buses on the special racegoers' route 406F were newly-hired red MB-types that year. Turning at Epsom Station MB19 (LH) shows off its ungainly length as well as its twin doors. It had originally been Red Arrow MBA19, but after only just over a year in that role was replaced by newer MBAs, fitted with seats in its former standee area, and used as a conventional O.M.O. bus. Note also the very nasty dent on the dreadful old thing's front registration plate! After the races, the MBs were farmed out to whichever London Country garages needed them to prop up services but, of course, they were just as unreliable there as they were in the former Central Area.

Two days later, on 7th June 1974, RTs and RFs still dominated the scene in Harlow New Town. In the evening rush hour, RT2504 (HA) has a standing load aboard on the 397A to Bishops Stortford, and escorts RF120 (HA) standing in for an RP on Green Line route 720's recent extension to Stansted Airport. They negotiate the roundabout at the junction of Fourth Avenue and Central Avenue.

Town Services in Harlow had recently been revised, resulting in such new routes as the 806, 807, 810 and 810A. RTs once again were very much in evidence - RT964 (HA) being on the latter also at the junction of Fourth Avenue and Central Avenue. In fact during this evening rush hour, I observed none of Harlow's RMLs at all, though two or three ANs were to be seen!

As well as special hospital services, London Country, like the old LT Country Area before it, operated various special routes for schools. Several of these were in the Watford Area, one being route 346D on which MBS279 (GR), one of the standee versions of these ill-fated vehicles that had entered service on local routes here in the spring of 1969, heads along Aldenham Road, Bushey on 20th June 1974.

Also in Aldenham Road, RML2421 (GR) has picked up a full load of pupils from the nearby Queens Schools, leaving many more behind - the RT just visible in the distance will probably clear them. Note how this RML does not have a via blind fitted for route 346C, an indication of how in some respects London Country was now getting sloppy in vehicle presentation. In addition, this is yet another RML that did not get a full overhaul when due in 1973, and was delicensed in February 1975 then cannibalised for spares. It too perished early in 1978.

Red MBs on loan from London Transport came to help out in the Watford area, too. Also on 20th June 1974, MB130 (GR) heads south along St. Albans Road near Watford Junction Station on route 318. Of note here is the non-LT style blind, another sign of the growing estrangement between London Country and London Transport.

On 16th July 1974, RFs are still very much in evidence at Stevenage. Not only were they subbing for RPs on routes 716 and 716A, but also still working many local routes. An example is downgraded modernised Green Line RF165 (SV) running out from Stevenage Garage to work a short journey on route 304 from Hitchin to Whitwell.

One of the busiest London Country routes was the 480, which ran from Denton, a suburb of Gravesend to Erith and had gained RMLs in the autumn of 1965. They would remain on the route until almost the end of LCBS Routemaster operation, and on 18th July 1974, RML2337 (NF) heads into Dartford bound for Erith. Despite having a full overhaul when seven years old, this RML also fell victim to the vehicle spares shortage in June 1975 and never ran again, going for scrap early in 1978.

Also in Dartford that day, modernised RF218 (NF) stands in for one of the underpowered SMAs on the southern peripheral Green Line route 725 and, in fact, still bears Green Line livery. It calls at Dartford Market Place; two of the box-like LT DMSs at route 96's terminus complete the picture.

A batch of RMCs were by this time based at Dartford Garage for local route 499, on which RMC1485 (DT) also passes the Market Place. When I took this photograph, I could never have imagined that this RMC would be working as a red bus on the X15 Docklands Express service fifteen years later!

A number of RFs were still active at Amersham Garage on local services in the autumn of 1974; indeed several of those that had been converted from Country buses to Green Line coaches in 1956, then back to Country buses again ten years later, were still there. One such, RF307 (MA), originally RF526, runs out from the garage to take up service on route 353 on 14th September 1974. However, new Bristol LHs of the BL and BN classes were beginning to replace them by now - one of them stands in the background. One of the ill-fated SMs is on the left.

On the same occasion, a well-filled modernised RF168 (MA), still in Green Line livery, passes the garage bound for Ley Hill on route 462. The original Amersham & District garage buildings may be seen behind the RF; the later 1930s London Transport structure is in the foreground. Alas, as with most Country Area garages, this splendid building is no more!

Above: Some of Harlow's New Town services, complete with RTs, were extended to Epping Station in rush hours. On the evening of 26th September 1974, RT1027 (HA) sets off from there on new route 807 for Harlow Town Station, which is some distance from the New Town. The three-line via blind, rather than the bland 'Town Service' display, is of note.

Right: Looking very shabby despite a repaint in NBC corporate livery eighteen months previously, RML2438 (GR) stands at Uxbridge Station awaiting the off on route 347A on 29th September 1974. Shortly afterwards, in October, it was delicensed, never to run again - yet another victim of the spares shortage which eventually perished in the Yorkshire scrapyards in January 1978.

By 6th November 1974, the unhappy RC class had been demoted to bus status, and exiled to Hertford Garage where they replaced RFs on route 390, which at that time ran from Sawbridgeworth via Harlow and Hertford to Stevenage. RC7 (HG) stands at the latter terminus. They would fare little better in this role, which was their last, apart from a few used as trainers.

Above: A combination of the desperate shortage of buses, and the more flexible working agreements London Country had with their staff, produced the remarkable spectacle of 39-seat modernised Green Line RF75 (EG) standing on for a 72-seat RML at West Croydon Bus Station on busy trunk route 409 on 18th February 1975! The RF, which usually stood in for SNC coaches on Green Line route 708, is painted in an odd livery of Lincoln Green with a white waistband, and NBC-style London Country logo above its windows. An RML side blind fortunately fits its front blind box, though no destination is shown. It was in fact running all the way through to Forest Row.

Above: By 19th April 1975, RMCs have begun to replace RTs on route 301, which still ran all the way from Aylesbury to Little Bushey. RMC1463 (HH) looks smart after its second overhaul when negotiating the roundabout at Beechen Grove, Watford. All was not well on this route, however, with RFs also having to be called upon to cover for missing double-deckers!

Left: The red MB-types are still at Watford, with standee MBS57 (GR) loading up, also at Beechen Grove, on route 346, which had received green examples of this type just over six years previously. The similar-looking vehicle following is a Harrow Weald-based MB on Central Area route 258. Having red buses working Country routes in areas like Watford where Central routes also ran must have confused passengers!

Red MBs did, however, work further out in the former Country Area. On 22nd April 1975, 50-seat conventional O.P.O. MB145 (MA) passes Amersham Station on route 362, once the preserve of ex-Green Line RTs.

An oddity to be found in the Amersham area at this time was SM476 (MA), adorned in an all-over livery for The Buckinghamshire Advertiser newspaper. It looked quite smart with its front and cab area painted dark blue, but unfortunately the lower corners have been scuffed - a problem common to the unwieldy MB and SM-types. Here, it collects passengers outside Amersham Garage on route 353 bound for Berkhamsted Station. Of note also is the LT bus stop flag affixed directly to the garage wall.

Approaching Berkhamsted itself, RMC1498 (HH) speeds along the A41 on route 312, where this type has recently replaced RTs - in theory at least! It appears to have a standing load aboard, perhaps homegoing commuters whom it has collected at Hemel Hempstead Station.

Hemel Hempstead Station is the setting for this view of modernised RF246 (HH), now downgraded to bus status, awaiting departure for Harpenden on cross-country route 307A. Before too long, such routes would be savagely cut back, or withdrawn altogether, hastening the end of these reliable old vehicles, and even the premature demise of newer types meant to replace them.

Packed to the gunwales, RF196 (HH) is one of at least two - both downgraded modernised Green Line examples - that have had to be pressed into service on the busy 301 owing to a shortage of RMCs and/or RTs during the evening rush hour of 22nd April 1975. It approaches Two Waters Garage.

Left: In contrast to the previous two pictures, modernised Green Line RFs 94 and 115 are two of a group parked outside Two Waters Garage awaiting disposal. Nevertheless, another four years would pass before the last London Country RF was withdrawn.

Below: Despite modernised Green Line RFs now being withdrawn, many unmodernised examples which had been downgraded to bus status in the mid-1960s were still going strong. Standing in for one of the Leyland Nationals that had replaced RFs two years previously on Green Line route 706, RF69 (CM) changes crew outside Two Waters Garage.

RTs were still going strong at Hemel Hempstead, too. RT2157 (HH) approaches the garage on route 320 on which, in common with the 301, 302 and 312, they were at this time freely intermixed with RMCs. This RT has since suffered the ignominy of being used for several years as an Estate Agent's office in Camden Town, after a spell in preservation!

In the Watford area RMCs were now being used to cover for missing RMLs on routes such as the 306 and 311. On 30th April 1975, RMC1495 (GR) stands at the traffic lights at Chalk Hill, Bushey working a 306 rush hour journey to Borehamwood, Ripon Way.

Under budding trees in The Avenue, Bushey, RT2779 (HH) heads for Hemel Hempstead on route 302, which paralleled the 301 between Two Waters and Little Bushey. Though no doubt intended, full RMC conversion of these two important trunk routes was never completed.

At Bushey Station in the evening rush hour, RML2424 (GR) on route 306 follows an RT on route 301. Some four years later, towards the end of RML operation by London Country, this RML and sister vehicle RML2423 were sold for scrap despite being in full working order, unlike the seventeen other RMLs which had been cannibalised, which also went for scrap in early 1978. Evidently this was because London Country were running out of storage space for redundant vehicles (mostly RM-types) and London Transport were haggling about the price for buying them all back. So perhaps the sale of these two unfortunate RMLs was merely for Schadenfreude at LT's expense? Whatever the case, not long after their untimely demise, London Transport did purchase all available London Country Routemasters, irrespective of condition!

As late as 2nd May 1975, a handful of RTs still operated rush hour journeys on route 303 between the Stevenage Industrial Area and Hitchin. In pouring rain, RT981 (SV), minus a number in its route-number blind box, picks workers up at Gunnells Wood Road in pouring rain. RTs had to be used on this route due to a railway bridge at Little Wymondley that was too low for an AN to safely negotiate, whereas an RT could do so. This particular RT was the last to operate in traditional Lincoln green livery. Regrettably, it has since been preserved in red livery, which it never carried in service!

Derby Day 4th June 1975 was the last time RTs worked special route 406F in any numbers, and a few red MBs and a couple of RFs helped out, as well as XF1 (EG). This departs from Epsom Station, and has been painted in NBC corporate livery, previously having carried London Country green and yellow, as applied to the first ANs.

During the summer of 1975, Staines Garage also had some of its RMLs off the road owing to the spares shortages, with RTs standing in for them. However on 11th July 1975, RML2413 (ST) is fit enough to run on route 441 all the way to High Wycombe. It has just run out from the garage and is on the recently-introduced ring road around the town centre. This RML would be the last to carry London Country livery some five years later when, after sale back to London Transport, it retained it when in use as a driver trainer, before being overhauled as a red bus and returned to service.

By 16th July 1975, so many RMLs were off the road at Garston Garage that routes 306 and 311 were as good as reverted to RT operation! RT4751 (GR) works a through journey of the 306 to New Barnet, with a red MB following it, at Bushey Station.

At Uxbridge Station on the same day, RF673 (HE) turns round in order to set off for its home town on route 305. MBs had replaced RTs on this route, but inevitably RFs had to stand in for them for several years. This one is in NBC corporate livery, and the advert on its side actually relieves the monotony of the all-over green!

Also on 16th July 1975, RML2458 (WR) passes through Iver Heath on route 457. Although overhauled when due in March 1973, this RML sadly expired in January 1977, and was yet another to perish a year later.

Windsor's RMLs are already in trouble now, since RT2722 (WR) has been sent there to cover for them. Here it passes The Black Horse pub in Iver, where I was enjoying a couple of pints at the time. Route 452 had been renumbered from route 457A, since Leyland Nationals then being delivered and ultimately expected to work these routes had three-track number blinds with no provision for a suffix.

Between Epping, Ongar and Brentwood, Country route 339 straddled the outer edge of the Central Area. On 26th July 1975, RTs are still going strong on the route as RT4783 (HA) passes the Robin Hood & Little John pub in Brentwood, which was the terminus both of Green Line route 721 and Central Area route 247. This would, however, be the RTs' last summer of a full allocation on the 339.

RFs and RTs, along with a few RMCs and RMLs, were still quite plentiful on Green Line reliefs on August Bank Holiday Monday 25th August 1975. RT4563 (HA) loads up working a Windsor-bound 718 at Marble Arch that day, and I wonder whether the family trying to get what looks like a non-folding pram onto the RT succeeded in doing so?

In the evening of the same day, RMC1488 (SJ) brings back racegoers from a Bank Holiday meeting at Brands Hatch on route 719 as it approaches Eccleston Bridge, Victoria. These former Green Line coaches were based at Swanley Garage for route 477 at the time, and would remain there until January 1980.

On 11th September 1975, one of two kept at Godstone for route 709, RCL2226 (GD) pulls out of Marlpit Lane, Couldson onto the Brighton Road, heading into town on that route. It still retains Green Line livery, complete with light green waistband and would do until bought back by London Transport in 1979.

Passing South Croydon Garage on 9th October 1975, the corporate N.B.C. livery of RCL2220 (RG) on a short journey of route 414 to Capel contrasts with the darker green and yellow earlier London Country livery on the RML following on route 409.

Above: A much more exotic vehicle working route 409 that day in Brighton Road, South Croydon is LS2 (GD), one of three ex-Southdown Northern Counties-bodied Leyland Titan PD3's acquired to help with vehicle shortages. It had been new in 1958 to Southdown, whose original green and cream livery it retained, and had been their No.933. The three Titans ran from Godstone Garage from July 1975 until May 1976. Somewhat bizarrely, at the time this picture was taken, other Leyland PD3s hired from Southend Corporation were running along the same stretch of road as them between West Croydon and Coulsdon on route 190!

Left: By 29th November 1975, not only were RTs still commonplace on the supposedly RMC-operated route 406, but even RF655 (RG), complete with conductor, has had to be pressed into service! It has just pulled away from the bus and coach stop at Reigate Station here.

On 10th January 1976, downgraded modernised Green Line RF108(GY) looks somewhat careworn as it arrives at the Purlfeet Station terminus of route 371A. Of note is the splendid old L.G.O.C.-style post holding the 'Buses Only' sign protecting the terminal stand on the left.

Remaining RFs and RTs were now being rapidly withdrawn, and on the same day this sad-looking group are awaiting disposal in the yard outside Grays Garage. Nearest the camera are RF692, on whose front the words 'All Clear' indicate that it has been stripped of re-usable parts (as may be observed by its missing headlamps), and RT3679 which appears to have suffered damage whilst being towed there.

RMC1496 (GY) heads into Romford past the bus stand at Corbets Tey, just east of Upminster, where RLHs once terminated on route 248A. Just discernable are the words 'Buses & Coaches Only' on the sign protecting it - Green Line coach route 722 used to terminate there, too. As for RMC1496, it was another to have a new lease of life in red on Docklands Express route X15 in 1989.

On 24th January 1976, RT3530 (GR) keeps route 347A going as RMLs continue to fall victim to the vehicle spares shortage. It heads along the Oxford Road passing London Transport's Central Area Uxbridge Garage, which was some distance outside Greater London - the outskirts of Uxbridge itself are visible in the distance. The garage was relocated and rebuilt adjacent to Uxbridge Station in 1984.

At Tilbury, Feenan Highway terminus on 28th February 1976, bound for Rainham on route 371, RF684 (GY) accompanies one of the increasing number of Leyland Nationals in the London Country fleet which were now rapidly sweeping away RFs, RTs and Routemasters alike. Of note is the typical London Transport Country Area bus shelter on the right, complete with 'Bus Stop' sign affixed to it, rather than to a bus stop post.

So desperate was the shortage of vehicles caused by difficulties in getting spare parts for them that London Country were now hiring vehicles from other operators than just London Transport. Across the Thames on the same day, Maidstone Corporation Massey-bodied Leyland Titan PD2 No.23 is one of a batch dating from the early 1960s, sent to Dartford Garage in place of RMCs for route 499. It stands at Joyce Green Hospital terminus. Livery of these vehicles was light blue and cream.

In the same area, Eastbourne Corporation A.E.C. Regent Vs with East Lancs bodywork, also dating from the early 1960s, were sent to Swanley Garage to cover for their missing RMCs. No.68, in a cream and dark blue livery, heads along Dartford High Street on route 477.

Both types of provincial vehicle stand together in the yard of Dartford Garage: two Maidstone Corporation Massey-bodied Titan PD2s, with No.16 on the right, accompany Eastbourne Regent V No.67. An SM may also be observed on the left.

Left· A more reassuring sight at Dartford Garage that day is recently repainted RML2324 (NF) which has terminated there on route 482, a variation of the traditional 480. With a BL, two SMs and two hired vehicles as a backdrop, this RML would return to London Transport when London Country had finished with it and last until the very end of normal Routemaster operation in London in December 2005!

Below: Illustrating the extremes London Country had to go to at this period to keep services going, little BN44 (DS), one of the small E.C.W.-bodied Bristol LHSs meant for lightly-trafficked Country routes, has had to be used as a Green Line relief on route 703 on 20th March 1976. It stands in Bessborough Gardens, Victoria. Route 703 had been introduced in May 1975 replacing most of the southern section of route 714, but did not last long. Nor did the little BN's, since many of the routes they were intended for were withdrawn amid savage cuts to rural services not long after their introduction.

Above: On the same day, former Ribble full-fronted Burlingham-bodied Leyland Titan PD3 LR6 (LH) approaches Victoria Station on driver training duties. Twenty of these 72-seaters were purchased by London Country for this purpose during 1975/76; their forward staircases being removed to enable an instructor to sit behind the driver. This had been Ribble No.1604 and was new in 1958. The last of these was withdrawn from these duties in 1980.

Left: On 1st April 1976, a number of RMCs and RCLs were still active on local routes in the Grays and Tilbury areas. RMC1507 (GY) heads along London Road, South Stifford on route 375. This RML, some five years later, would somewhat oddly, after passing to London Transport, and being used for driver training for a year or so, be sold privately for preservation.

RMC2241 departs from East Purfleet, Thames Board Mills terminus, leaving two RMCs on the stand. Although showing a blind for route 328, it is apparently actually working the related route 329. It is still in its original Green Line livery, but with London Country fleetname.

On route 374, more usually operated by RFs at this period, RCL2246 (GY) crosses Tank Hill Road bridge in Purfleet. This one is also still in original Green Line livery.

Modernised Green Line RF88 (GY), now demoted to bus status but painted in N.B.C. corporate dual-purpose livery, has arrived at the Aveley, Usk Road terminus of route 371B. This area was originally a London Country Council 'out-county' estate, which is why the houses visible in the background are similar to those on the Becontree Estate.

RCL2237 (GD) was unique in being the only London Country Routemaster to carry N.B.C. corporate livery with a Green Line fleetname. In the evening rush hour of 12th April 1976, it heads for home along Upper Regent Street. Three RCLs were retained for this route at Godstone Garage; the last - this one - ran just over a month later on 14th May.

On Easter Monday, 19th April 1976, RP77 (SA) unusually finds itself working a Bank Holiday Green Line extra on route 713 to Whipsnade Zoo. It loads up at Golders Green Station, and also carries N.B.C. dual purpose livery. The 713 was usually SNC operated at this time; the RP was one of St. Albans' allocation for route 727.

At West Croydon Bus Station on 28th April 1976, Bournemouth Corporation 1965 Alexander-bodied Daimler Fleetline No.195 contrasts with a London Country AN, dating from 1972, and an RML. These Fleetlines had originally been hired in the autumn of 1975. By coincidence, a batch of similar vehicles, but with detachable tops, was bought by London Transport for its Round London Sightseeing Tour in the autumn of 1977.

By this time, the busy 403 running between Wallington and Warlingham was the last major Country route to be substantially RT-operated. RT3461 (CM) passes along Tamworth Road, Croydon.

COUNTRY COUSINS

Just over three weeks later, some RMCs have moved across the river from Grays to Chelsham Garage to start replacing RTs on route 403. On 21st May 1976, RMC1472 (CM) nestles under the trees at The Old Ship, Tastfield to where odd school journeys of the route were extended.

In the hot summer of 1976, traditional ex-London Transport vehicles still appeared on Green Line relief duties. On 11th June that year, RML2453 (ST) has a long way to go when passing Hampton Court on its way to Harlow on route 718.

Long after their official replacement on southern peripheral Green Line route 725, RF202 (NF) speeds along Staines Road West, Ashford on 17th July 1976. It is still in Green Line livery, and will eventually be the last RF in normal service, outliving the last red RFs by several weeks in the spring of 1979.

Another modernised RF still active at this time is RF183 (ST), now painted in light green and yellow bus livery. It passes along Staines High Street the same day. It is noteworthy that both RFs are running with their platform doors open, no doubt due to the very hot weather!

In the spring and summer of 1976, the Southend Corporation Leyland Titan PD3's which had been loaned to London Transport and used at Croydon on route 190 during the winter of 1975/76 were loaned to London Country, where they took over from RTs on route 339 at Harlow Garage. Massey-bodied No.336, dating from 1965, heads along Epping High Street on 21st August 1976.

Above: With an MBS in pursuit, RT4792 (HG) climbs up Victoria Street in St. Albans substituting for an RMC on route 341. An RMC side blind is fitted to its via box, in similar fashion to those on red RTs also covering for missing RM-types at this period in the Central Area.

Right: By 5th February 1977, route 339 had been converted to RML operation. RML2353 (HA) climbs out of Epping on its way to its home town. After many more years use as a red bus than it had had as a green one, this RML has ended up preserved in Australia!

Below: A surprise in the late spring of 1977 was the repainting of three RTs in full N.B.C. corporate livery for use at Chelsham Garage, even though route 403 was now largely RMC and RCL-operated. On 1st June 1977, an immaculate RT1018 (CM) shows off its new livery on local route 453, though the blind display using a torn destination blind and an RMC side-blind spoils things somewhat! And Caterham Station still has its Southern Electric and early British Railways signage.

Other odd vehicles at work from Chelsham Garage at this time were some Massey-bodied Leyland Atlanteans dating from 1965 which were loaned by Maidstone Corporation to keep route 403 going. No.30 deposits passengers in Sussex Road, South Croydon.

1st June 1977 was also Derby Day, and was the last time that traditional ex-London Transport vehicles dominated the special 406F race service. Many of them, including RCL2234 departing from Epsom Station, were former Green Line Routemaster coaches which were expellees from the recent O.P.O. conversion of route 370 at Grays, though one of the N.B.C.-liveried RTs from Chelsham, and a couple of Leyland Nationals also turned out.

It will soon be the turn of London Country's crew-operated trunk routes radiating from Croydon to convert to O.P.O. On 28th June 1977, this busy scene shows RCL2244 (DS) bound for distant Horsham on the 414 leading a red RM through South End. An RML on route 409 and a new Leyland National, which has just entered service on route 12A, complete the picture: above them flags and decorations are out for H.M. Queen Elizabeth II's Silver Jubilee.

A little further south, a packed RML2312 (GD) appears not to be sure whether it is a 411 or a 414 - it is actually a 411, and has a canopy blind fitted to the front number box. This typifies the sloppy blind displays often to be seen on Routemasters in their final months with London Country. Many of those displaced by O.P.O. vehicles at this stage went into store, once Chelsham and Swanley had their full complement of them, though most would eventually be 'repatriated' to London Transport. What a contrast between the pleasant design of the RML, and the box-like DMS - the latter matches the awful 1950s/1960s office blocks in the background!

Despite the three N.B.C.-liveried RTs, Chelsham will have its full complement of RMCs and RCLs for the 403 once routes 405 and 414 lose the latter, and one of those already there is RCL2218 (CM). This speeds past the Swan & Sugar Loaf pub, once a London bus terminus and now sadly converted to a Tesco's, on one of the 403's Express journeys.

By 16th July 1977, many of the Routemasters that had been off the road for up to three years as a result of the vehicle spares shortage in the mid-1970s, had been badly cannibalised to keep others in service. Several were assembled in the yard at Grays Garage, where RML2337, 2421, 2427 and 2345 make a sorry sight. All have their engines missing, as well as various other components. Most will never run again, though one of these four will have a last-minute escape, as will be explained later!

More defunct Routemasters, RML2306, RMC1505 and RML2320 accompany T1 (102PKP) in the yard of Grays Garage on the same occasion. The latter is an early 1960s Harrington Wayfarer-bodied A.E.C. Reliance coach that had been acquired from Maidstone & District for training duties. The plight of these unfortunate vehicles was worsened by the attention of vandals, who have already aimed missiles at the rear windows of the two RMLs and an RF on the extreme right.

At this period, two new Green Line routes, the 702 and 703 running from Walthamstow Central and Waltham Cross respectively to Bishops Stortford via Epping and Harlow had replaced the traditional 718 and 720. Although officially allocated RPs, they were often worked by RMLs based at Harlow for the 339. On 16th August 1977, RML2353 (HA) has just passed a red RT on route 217A in Shernbroke Road on the new G.L.C. 'out-county' Ninefields Estate near Waltham Cross. Four days later, the 217A was withdrawn, leaving the 703 sole service provider here.

A much odder appearance of an RML on the same day is that of RML2347 (HG) standing in for an AN on route 316 when negotiating the roundabout at the junction of the Great Cambridge Road and Bullsmoor Lane. Route 316 had never been Routemaster-operated, having been renumbered from the old route 310A. By now, odd Routemasters were allocated as spares to cover for missing O.P.O. vehicles at various London Country garages, as has happened here. This RML, nearly twenty-eight years later, would have the dubious 'honour' of being the last Routemaster home on route 19, which I have known since early childhood!

By a remarkable coincidence, N.B.C.-liveried RT1018 (CM) working route 403 and RF125 (WR) on the 725 appear together at West Croydon Bus Station on 7th September 1977. By now, few survivors of both types remain in service with London Country. Of the three RTs in this livery at Chelsham, this one and RT3461 were demoted to training duties a few days later, leaving RT604 to soldier on until April 1978. However, RT981 still in Lincoln green also lasted at Reigate Garage until February that year. Two Country Routemasters are also just visible on the left, too.

One of the latter, RCL2248 (CM) has just called on its journey from Chelsham to Warlingham and, oddly, has recently received a new blind display with upper-case via points, harking back to pre-1961 displays, long before this RCL was built! These would have another year or so in use on route 403.

A pocket of RML operation remained at Staines and Windsor on 26th September 1977, perhaps because the railway bridge over South Street in Staines was too low for an AN to pass beneath, whereas an RML just managed it, as RML2415 (WR) shows. It is actually working route 441 - the 441B was a local route in the Slough area. The final solution to this problem was to convert the route to single-deck Leyland Nationals, as also happened to red bus route 117 which ran under the bridge too.

Four days later, on 30th September 1977, RML2413 (WR) departs from the grotesque new bus station in Slough on route 458, which for many years had been the preserve of RFs. A number of local routes here still had RMLs working them, often interworked with one another, including route 407 on which they lingered on into 1980.

The last major crew operation in the former northern Country Area was that of RMCs on routes 330 and 341. On 18th October 1977, a month of so before their conversion to O.P.O., RMC1498 heads through Fleetville on its way from Welwyn Garden City to Hemel Hempstead. By now, rumours were rife that the growing number of redundant London Country Routemasters would return to London Transport: they were true, and this was one of the first to do so, just two months later. It became a driver trainer for LT in January 1978.

A rogue working on route 341 (or is it 341B?) is that of Garston's RML2431 standing in for an RMC. It is on its way from Hertford to St. Albans when passing Fleetville School.

A couple of days before O.P.O. conversion, RMC1517 (HF) represents the final official allocation of crew-operated vehicles to route 341. It speeds towards the village of Smallford, passing a nice old L.T. Country Area bus stop and wooden shelter.

The last RT to operate in the original Lincoln green livery, with cream waistband, was RT981. With an SM and two hired Bournemouth Fleetlines for company, it stands outside Leatherhead Garage on 21st January 1978 between duties on route 406, which was still RMC-operated at the time. The RT worked up to Kingston on this route in the evening rush hour, and was demoted to training duties a few days later. Unfortunately, although preserved, this historic RT is wrongly restored in red livery, which it never carried in service!

By 4th March 1978, route 480 was one of the last former Country routes to be fully RML operated. Many of them had become very shabby, literally in many shades of green! This is shown by RML2343 (NF) passing through Northfleet. Of note also is the N.B.C.-style bus stop flag: these are finally replacing traditional London Transport ones more than eight years after LT's loss of Country Area and Green Line services.

In the same area, route 477 was also one of the last to be fully RMC operated. On 4th March 1978 too, RMC1493 (SJ) has terminated at its home garage, Swanley. On the left stands a new Leyland National which has recently replaced the SMs that had only replaced RTs on route 423 in the spring of 1972.

Although they were building up a large fleet of Leyland Nationals, London Country also had a new batch of Leyland Atlanteans delivered in 1978. On 24th April 1978, brand new AN128 (LH) has just changed driver in Leatherhead, bound for Dorking on route 470. This was one of sixty single-door examples bodied by Park Royal; a further one hundred Roe-bodied vehicles of similar design followed. They would, in effect, finish off London Country's remaining Routemasters in early 1980.

By the spring of 1978, the unhappy RC class had all been withdrawn from service. Some were used as driver trainers, in which capacity RC13 passes through Southborough on 4th May 1978.

On 26th July 1978, RMC1485 (SJ) negotiates a three-point turn in the Kentish village of Crockenhill on an afternoon school journey that terminated there. This turn, which would have been difficult for O.P.O. vehicles, was one of the reasons why route 477 retained crew operation for so long.

Although still fully blinded in the yard of Chelsham Garage on 23rd August 1978, RCL2234 (CM) has recently been withdrawn. The other RCL on the left is RCL2220, which has already been out of use for six months. Both will languish in store until rescued by London Transport, and will eventually re-enter services as red buses in North London in the latter half of 1980. The defunct RT behind the RCLs is RT1563, still in use as a uniform store.

On the same day as the previous picture was taken, RMC1475 (LH) crosses Epsom Downs on route 406. The days of former Green Line coach Routemasters on both the 403 and 406 were now numbered, with more new ANs being delivered to replace them. The 403 Express, however, retained them for a few months longer, whilst route 477 would be the last of all, lingering on until January 1980.

Above: By 10th September 1978, route 726, a variant of the southern peripheral Green Line coach route 725, had been introduced between Windsor and Gravesend that served Heathrow Airport, where SMA5 (WR) accompanies an Aldervalley Leyland National. These smart-looking but underpowered A.E.C. Swifts were now virtually clapped out, and would not last much longer. However a shortened version of route 726 survives at the time of writing as as London Buses service X26 and has recently been double-decked.

Centre: A very late appearance of an RML on route 411 is that of RML2313 (RG) on 13th September 1978. Flanked by two London Country Leyland Nationals, which by now have ousted most Routemasters which worked here, it sports a very odd-looking via blind as it sets off for Godstone from West Croydon Bus Station.

Bottom: Despite the replacement of RMCs in the Hatfield and Welwyn areas in the autumn of 1977, a couple of them were retained at Hatfield Garage as spare cover for O.P.O. vehicles. By the autumn of 1978, local routes serving Welwyn Garden City had been numbered in the G series, and for some reason RMC1512 (HF) was a regular performer on route G4. Complete with a very rudimentary blind display, RMC1512 turns from Moors Walk into Panshanger Road, in a part of the garden city yet to be developed, on 15th September 1978.

Another isolated pocket of surviving Routemaster operation in the former Country Area at this period was on New Town route 808 at Harlow, where RML2352 (HA) approaches its terminus at Katherines also on 15th September 1978. This area too has yet to be fully developed, and new building work may be seen on the right.

A handful of RMCs and RCLs survived at this period at Grays, too. They were usually employed on schools journeys, on which RCL2251, still in Lincoln green livery, passes The Cross Keys pub in Chadwell St. Mary on 15th September 1978.

Illustrating now London Country is by now getting further 'divorced' from its London Transport heritage, RN1 (DS) is one of a number of Plaxton 'Panorama'-bodied A.E.C. Reliance coaches acquired from fellow N.B.C. operator Trent Barton for school and private hire work. However, they sometimes appeared on Green Line route 714, on which RN1 calls at Hyde Park Corner on its way to Victoria on 26th October 1978.

Left & Centre: By the spring of 1979, London Country had so many defunct vehicles that they ran out of garage space to store them. Therefore they hired a disused airfield at Radlett for the purpose. On 19th May 1979, these views taken from the other side of the track of the Midland main line shows that not only were Routemasters, of all three types, involved, but also RPs and ANs dating only from 1972. Most of the Routemasters would return to service as red buses with London Transport - eventually.

Some of the eight 'experimental' XFs purchased in 1965 turned out to be some of the very last ex-London Transport vehicles in London Country use. On 24th May 1979, XF3 (EG) passes The Cherry Tree pub in Copthorne on their original route, the 424.

Above: The last ex-LT vehicle of all with London Country would be RF202 (NF), which on the same day as the previous picture was taken was already the last RF in normal service with both London Country and London Transport, the latter's having bowed out at the end of March 1979. It heads along Church Road, Hartley on local Gravesend area route 490, which it interworked with route 489. Interestingly, it is in N.B.C.-style Green Line livery. Subsequently, it was restored in L.T. Green Line livery and used on special 'ramblers' services' for a couple of years, prior to being preserved.

Right: Of the withdrawn Routemasters shown at Grays earlier in this book, all went for scrap early in 1978, except for RML2345. This had been so badly cannibalised that it was immobile, so it remained dumped there. By 4th July 1979, when this picture of it was taken surrounded by defunct more modern single-deckers, it had lost virtually all of its mechanical parts, its front blind-box, front upper deck windows and dome, as well as various other windows and internal fittings. Eventually, it was towed away on a low-loader when bought back by London Transport in November 1979. It May 1981, it emerged from Aldenham Works as good as new, and remained in service as a red bus until July 2005!

Below: RML2423 and 2424, which had expired at Garston Garage in September 1978 were not so lucky as RML2345. Despite being in full running order, both were sold to Wombwell Diesels (who had also scrapped the seventeen RMLs, two RMCs and two RCLs, which had been cannibalised, early in 1978) for scrap in April 1979. It seems that London Transport were haggling about the price of London Country's dozens of redundant Routemasters, which were incurring storage charges at Radlett Aerodrome or clogging up their garage space, so they were sold for scrap merely for Schadenfreude! The move did force LT's hand, since during the summer, all stored Country RMLs, RMCs and RCLs were snapped up by them, as were those still in use once they were made redundant. The unfortunate RML2423 is reduced to this skeletal state at Wombwell on 5th July 1979.

Above: A small pocket of RML operation survived at Windsor Garage throughout 1979, primarily for use on Slough local route 407. However, they also made forays onto their old haunts such as route 457, on which RML2411 (WR) passes through Uxbridge Common on 30th August 1979. The tower blocks in Uxbridge Town Centre are visible in the distance on the left, spoiling an otherwise purely rural scene.

Left: On 1st October 1979, SM476 (DT) looks quite smart when working local route 499 in Dartford Town Centre, having been overhauled early in 1978. However, by this time many of this unfortunate class had already been withdrawn, and this one, part of a batch of ninety Metro-Cammell-bodied examples new only in 1971, was withdrawn in the summer of 1980. All had followed suit by the end of 1981.

An odd outpost of final Routemaster operation for London Country was route 493, which ran entirely within the London Borough of Bromley in the Orpington area, and had been numbered 854 until the spring of 1967. On 21st October, 1979, RMC1512 (SJ) heads along Cheslfield Lane on its loop working. This RMC would be the last in London Country service a few weeks later, on route 477 which interworked with the 493 from Swanley Garage.

Illustrating how Green Line vehicles continued to work on Country bus routes in London Country's 'post-LT' area, Leyland National SNC181 (SJ) stands outside Dartford Garage on 9th December 1979 whilst working route 401.

On the same day, route 480 has recently fallen to these by now ubiquitous vehicles. SNB333 (NF) arrives at Joyce Green Hospital on a Sunday working of this previously RML-operated trunk route.

In 1971, fifteen A.E.C. Swifts were acquired by London Country from South Wales Transport, forming the SMW class. The first three had been new in 1969 and had Willowbrook dual-door bodywork, and worked from Crawley Garage. The other twelve had single-door Marshall bodies and were actually a diverted order from South Wales. These worked from St. Albans Garage, where SMW5 (SA) stands on 15th December 1979. This was one of the last SMWs to be withdrawn, in April 1981.

Some of London Country's SMs limped on into 1980 without having been overhauled, and still bearing their original Lincoln green Livery. One such is SM514 (DT) on local route 494 in Hythe Street, Dartford, about to be overtaken by RMC1485 (SJ) on the 477 on 12th January 1980. The latter is now due for imminent replacement by new ANs.

A week later on 19th January 1980, brand new AN219 (SJ) stands at Azalea Drive, Swanley, having just entered service to replace RMC's on route 477. The conversion was a gradual one, so it is working with a conductor until all the RMCs have gone.

COUNTRY COUSINS

Route 407 at Slough was one of the last outposts of London Country RML operation. On a very gloomy 26th January 1980, RML2422 (WR) heads out of Langley Village bound for Cippenham, which was the westernmost extremity of London Country operation in the Slough area.

On 1st March 1980, London Country organised a Farewell Tour for their last Routemasters. It was operated by RML2446 (NF) and RMC1512 (SJ). As they climb Sanderstead Hill, their badly dented front domes typify the neglected appearance these buses had in their last years, and also the spelling of the word 'ROUTMASTER' on their blinds is decidedly odd! Both were immediately sold to London Transport after this tour, the RMC being used for several years for driver training, and the RML overhauled as a red bus. It remained in service until March 2004, and is now preserved in red.

London Country made somewhat belated efforts in the late 1970s to improve Green Line's image. The route network was radically altered, and new coaches delivered. These were 'proper' coaches, as opposed to the previous RF, RC and RP types which were more correctly described as dual-purpose vehicles. Most of the new vehicles were A.E.C. Reliances with either Duple (RB class) or Plaxton (RS class) bodies, but two Volvo's with Duple bodies were also purchased. The first of these, DV1 (HG) heading along Wood Green High Road on 5th April 1980, typifies the 'new order', working new Green Line route 734, which followed the existing 715 from Hertford to Wood Green, then meandered its way through north and west London, serving such places as Brent Cross Shopping Centre and Heathrow Airport before ending up at Addlestone. Unfortunately, this route was sabotaged by murderous traffic congestion so did not last long. In this view, DV1 carries the special livery marking Green Line's Golden Jubilee.

Left: An open day was held at London Country's Stevenage Garage in connection with Green Line's Golden Jubilee on 17th May 1980. One of the exhibits was N.B.C.-liveried RT1018, which was still in use as a driver trainer and, since it still had a certificate of fitness, gave rides to spectators. Here it has deposited some of them outside the garage. It was to be the last RT in London Country stock, sold in October 1981 and preserved in this livery.

Below: Passing the garage on the same occasion, RP10 (HF) has been demoted to bus duties and had its Green Line fleetname painted out. It heads for Hitchin on route 300.

To make room for a display of vehicles at Stevenage Garage, a number of vehicles housed there were parked at nearby Monks Wood. One of them is defunct Leyland National LN3, which along with the SM behind it had been working Superbus services. It had latterly been in use as an engineering training vehicle, and although later resuscitated as a driver trainer, never ran in service again.

At the main special event commemorating Green Line's Golden Jubilee, held on 13th July 1980 at London Country's Crawley overhaul works, new AN228 (CY) works special route C50 which has been laid on to ferry visitors to and from Crawley Bus Station.

A less salubrious vehicle at the event is DMS631, one of a few of that unfortunate class which London Country have recently bought from London Transport for use as driver trainers. At least it looks smart in their N.B.C. livery. An array of Green Line coaches, past and present, are on show behind it.

After its retirement from normal bus duties, RF202 (DG), the last of its class in service, was used during the summer of 1980 on special 'Ramblers Bus' route 418. Restored to 1967 LT Green Line livery, it pauses in the Kentish village of Brasted on 24th August 1980. For some reason, it wrongly displays side-boards for Green Line route 701!

An oddity to be working route 757, one of London Country's new generation of Green Line routes usually operated by their 'proper' coaches, is RP10 (SA). With a makeshift blind display, it heads up Park Lane on 15th August 1981.

Above: At C.F. Booth's Rotherham scrapyard on 5th October 1981, XF2 makes a sad sight as it awaits cutting up. However, fellow Fleetline XF3 remained in service until January 1982, gaining the distinction of being the last ex-London Transport double-decker in service with London Country. Along with XF1, it is now preserved.

Left: A group of London Country's unloved SMs have also come to the end of the road at Booth's, along with some of their last MBSs and even a couple of Leyland Nationals. The RT just visible behind is RT4496, which had been one of London Country's last RT trainers.

An odd occurrence in April 1982 was the swap of routes 84 and 313 between London Transport and London Country. Much of the latter ran within Greater London, whilst most of route 84 ran in Hertfordshire. On the last day of route 313's operation by London Country, 23rd April 1982, Green Line coach RS15 (SA) most oddly works it, and with driver Christopher Sullivan at the wheel, calls at The White Hart, South Mimms.

In complete contrast, little Bristol LHS BN54 (SA) is also out on the 313 that day, in open country between South Mimms and London Colney. Upon takeover by London Transport, the 313 was withdrawn between Potters Bar and St. Albans, and replaced by a diversion of the 84. However, in September 1982 it was extended at its other end, from Enfield to Chingford, and still operates there today.

The first new double-deckers delivered to London Country were the eleven-strong AF class, which were 72-seat Northern Counties-bodied Daimler Fleetlines. They entered service, replacing RMLs on route 410 from Godstone Garage, in February 1972. On 2nd June 1982, AF2 (GD) stands outside the garage, having worked the 411. Four months later, the last AF was withdrawn from service, though a few lasted a little longer on training duties.

A strike by British Railways staff on 9th July 1982 led to many Green Line reliefs being operated, often using ordinary service buses. One of London Country's newest, Leyland Olympian LR5 (SA), is about to run around the block from Buckingham Palace Road to Eccleston Bridge at Victoria, working route 757 to Luton.

Similarly employed that day is AN9 (SV), heading along Ebury Street, Victoria to take up service on route 758 to Hemel Hempstead, complete with branding for the Stevenage Bus services it usually works.